CASE STUDIES
Applying Educational Psychology

Second Edition

Jeanne Ellis Ormrod
University of Northern Colorado (Emerita)
University of New Hampshire

Dinah Jackson McGuire
Buncombe County Schools, North Carolina

with contributions from

Linda L. Pallock
Cleveland State University

and

Brian E. Harper
Cleveland State University

PEARSON

**Merrill
Prentice Hall**

Upper Saddle River, New Jersey
Columbus, Ohio

Library of Congress Cataloging-in-Publication Data

Ormrod, Jeanne Ellis.
  Case studies : applying educational psychology / Jeanne Ellis Ormrod, Dinah
Jackson McGuire ; with contributions by Linda L. Pallock and Brian E. Harper.
    p. cm.
ISBN 0-13-198046-7 (pbk.)
  1. School psychology—United States—Case studies.   2. Educational
psychology—United States—Case studies.   I. McGuire, Dinah Jackson.
II. Pallock, Linda L.   III. Harper, Brian E.   IV. Title.   V. Title: Applying
educational psychology.
LB1027.55.J33 2007
371.4—dc22

                                                              2006016916

Vice President and Executive Publisher:
  Jeffery W. Johnston
Publisher: Kevin M. Davis
Editorial Assistant: Sarah N. Kenoyer
Production Editor: Mary Harlan
Production Coordination: Thistle Hill
  Publishing Services, LLC

Design Coordinator: Diane Lorenzo
Cover Designer: Ali Mohrman
Cover Image: Workbook Stock
Production Manager: Laura Messerly
Director of Marketing: David Gesell
Marketing Manager: Amy Judd
Marketing Coordinator: Brian Mounts

This book was set in Times by Integra Software Services. It was printed and bound by
R. R. Donnelley & Sons Company. The cover was printed by R. R. Donnelley & Sons Company.

Pearson Education Ltd.
Pearson Education Singapore Pte. Ltd.
Pearson Education Canada, Ltd.
Pearson Education–Japan

Pearson Education Australia Pty. Limited
Pearson Education North Asia Ltd.
Pearson Educación de Mexico, S.A. de C.V.
Pearson Education Malaysia Pte. Ltd.

V036   10 9
ISBN 0-13-198046-7

PREFACE

Future teachers can better understand and apply principles of educational psychology and related disciplines when they have numerous opportunities to see such principles in action. In this book we present classroom scenarios that illustrate a wide variety of phenomena related to development, learning, motivation, diversity, and classroom practice. Accompanying each scenario are questions encouraging readers to look beneath the surface of classroom events and consider how various concepts and theoretical perspectives might enhance understanding and offer possible strategies and interventions.

At the core of all the cases in this book are true stories, but we've often changed details to maintain confidentiality and enhance readability. My coauthor, Dinah Jackson McGuire, contributed many of the cases from her years of experience as a teacher in the early elementary and junior high school grades, and (later) from her work with children and adolescents with special educational needs. Some of the cases came from my own middle school classes or were based on my work as a school psychologist or supervisor of teacher interns. Still others came from professional colleagues. We are especially indebted to Barbara Day, Debby Grubbs, and an anonymous friend for the time they gave us in describing their experiences and observations.

The second edition adds five new cases to the collection, including three at the preschool level: "The Bully" (Case 1), "Haley and Meredith" (Case 5), "Animal Shelters" (Case 27), "I Bit My Tongue" (Case 28), and "The Unmotivated Student" (Case 39). The 48 cases are grouped into four general categories—child and adolescent development, learning and cognition, motivation and classroom management, and instruction and assessment—but all have relevance to two or more of these areas (see the matrix immediately following the table of contents).

Also new to the second edition are additional questions for the 43 cases from the first edition, with a focus on questions that mimic those that future teachers are apt to find on state licensure exams. I am deeply indebted to Linda Pallock and Brian Harper at Cleveland State University, who suggested many of the new questions. Linda and Brian have been using the first edition for some time now and often saw things in the cases that I myself had overlooked. Their perspectives and suggestions have enriched the book in innumerable ways.

Most of the cases have been field-tested in classes in educational psychology and related disciplines. Students' responses to them have been overwhelmingly positive. The following comments are typical of the feedback we've received:

"They [the case studies] make me feel like I am in the classroom."

"The case studies help me focus on the main topics in the textbook. They help make the textbook more real—like what actual teachers would see."

"It's easy to see how the theories work when I read the case studies. It makes me feel like a real teacher, and this class isn't some hoop that I have to get through to get my degree."

Accompanying the book is an *Instructor's Manual* that offers possible responses to the questions for each case. Instructors can obtain a copy of this manual by contacting their local Prentice Hall representative or calling Prentice Hall Customer Service at 1-800-922-0579.

I hope that my readers—instructors and students alike—find the book helpful. I'm always eager to hear your comments and suggestions. The easiest way to reach me is via email: jormrod@alumni.brown.edu

Jeanne Ellis Ormrod

CONTENTS

Instruction and Assessment

Matrix of Cases

Column groups: **Child and Adolescent Development** (Cognitive/Linguistic Development, Sense of Self, Social-Emotional/Moral Development); **Learning and Cognition** (Behaviorism/Social Cognition, Information Processing/Social Cognitive Theory, Complex Cognitive Processing/Constructivism); **Motivation and Classroom Management** (Motivation, Affect/Emotions, Classroom Management); **Instruction and Assessment** (Planning and Instruction, Assessment); **Diversity** (Individual and Group Differences, Special Educational Needs).

	Preschool	K–2	3–5	6–8	9–12	Cognitive/Linguistic Development	Sense of Self	Social-Emotional/Moral Development	Behaviorism/Social Cognition	Information Processing/Social Cognitive Theory	Complex Cognitive Processing/Constructivism	Motivation	Affect/Emotions	Classroom Management	Planning and Instruction	Assessment	Individual and Group Differences	Special Educational Needs
1. The Bully	x							x						x				
2. Learning the Ropes		x				x		x	x	x				x				
3. The Paycheck		x				x		x		x								
4. The Goldfish		x				x		x										
5. Haley and Meredith		x					x	x	x				x	x				
6. Houses and Boats			x			x		x			x				x			
7. The Art Box			x					x						x				
8. The Emergency Telephone Call			x					x	x					x				
9. Friends			x					x	x					x				
10. Alabama			x					x						x			x	
11. Studying French				x		x	x			x	x	x			x			
12. Pollution				x		x	x	x	x	x		x						
13. The Reflection in the Window	x					x		x	x					x				
14. The Marble Jar	x							x				x		x			x	x
15. Seven Chips			x					x	x		x			x				x
16. Throwing Tantrums			x			x	x		x					x	x			x
17. The Distracting Influence			x					x	x		x	x		x	x			
18. A Silent World			x						x					x	x			x
19. Topography				x						x	x	x			x			
20. Consequences				x				x	x					x				
21. Keeping Track of Business				x							x			x		x		x
22. Solving Problems				x					x	x	x				x	x		
23. First Aid				x		x				x	x				x	x		
24. The Respiratory System					x					x	x			x	x		x	

	Preschool	K-2	3-5	6-8	9-12	Child and Adolescent Development	Cognitive/Linguistic Development	Sense of Self	Social-Emotional/Moral Development	Learning and Cognition	Behaviorism/Social Cognitive Theory	Information Processing/Social Cognitive Theory	Complex Cognitive Processes	Motivation and Classroom Management	Motivation	Affect/Emotions	Classroom Management	Instruction and Assessment	Planning and Instruction	Assessment	Diversity	Individual and Group Differences	Special Educational Needs
25. The Concept Maps				x			x		x		x			x	x								
26. Coming Back to School				x		x			x										x	x		x	
27. Animal Shelters	x					x								x				x					
28. I Bit My Tongue	x								x	x							x						
29. Letters		x				x				x							x		x			x	
30. The Star Chart	x								x	x		x		x	x								
31. The Bulletin Board		x						x		x				x						x			
32. Halloween		x															x		x	x	x		
33. Culture Shock		x				x				x							x		x	x	x		
34. Getting a Drink		x							x					x	x	x							x
35. Summer School		x						x	x								x						x
36. Math Baseball			x			x	x							x	x			x					
37. The Stand-Up Comic			x				x	x	x								x						
38. The Perfectionist			x			x				x								x					x
39. The Unmotivated Student				x										x		x		x					x
40. Proofreading				x		x				x							x						
41. Cheerleading Tryouts			x						x					x	x								
42. The Morning Routine	x									x	x						x						
43. Horses and Aliens		x								x	x			x									
44. Endangered Species		x								x	x			x									
45. Climate			x			x				x	x						x	x		x			
46. The Research Paper			x			x								x	x								
47. The Pearl				x		x				x							x	x					
48. Under the Bleachers				x				x						x				x					

viii

CASE 1
The Bully

Ms. Knowles and Ms. Brophy co-teach a prekindergarten class for 4- and 5-year-olds. To some degree their class works on basic foundations of literacy and mathematics—identifying alphabet letters and their sounds, counting small sets of objects, and so on. But they are well aware that to be truly successful in elementary school, children must know how to work and play effectively with their peers. Accordingly, many of the class's daily activities are designed to nurture social development.

The two teachers use a variety of strategies for helping their young students acquire social skills and make friends. They suggest that outgoing and socially self-confident children ask more reserved children to join a play activity. They teach shy children how to ask "Can I play?" or to suggest ways in which they might contribute to an activity ("You already have a mommy, a daddy, and a baby. Can I be the big sister?"). They encourage children to watch for clues in one another's body language ("Look at Ivan's face. How do you think he feels about what you've just done?"). They sometimes bring two or three unengaged children together to work jointly on a project or puzzle. At story time, they read stories exploring the qualities that make for good friendships and the kinds of behaviors that are apt to alienate others. And they suggest that parents occasionally invite their children's classmates for lunch or a short play date.

Often the topic of friends comes up at "circle time," a part of each day when everyone gathers on the floor at the front of the room to discuss issues of general concern. In one circle time session, the teachers read a letter they say they received from their friend Mr. Stone, who lives in California. (In fact, there is no Mr. Stone. The teachers have written the letter themselves to facilitate a discussion about making friends.) "My daughter Susie doesn't have any friends," Mr. Stone allegedly writes. "Do you have any suggestions about how she could make friends?" The children offer a variety of suggestions for Susie Stone: "She could be nice to people." "She could find somebody who likes to play with Care Bears like she does." "Other kids could ask her if she wants to play with them."

Clearly, then, some of the children are acquiring social competencies that will serve them well in the elementary school years. Others lag behind, however. One child who still has much to learn is a handsome young 4-year-old named Liam. The son of two high-achieving college professors, Liam has a good start in academic skills; for instance, he can already read simple storybooks and solve addition problems involving one-digit numbers. But he has little knowledge about how to interact effectively with his peers. Rather than politely ask if he can join an ongoing activity, he is apt to bully his way into the situation, perhaps giving orders, snatching a desired toy, or making threats ("If you don't play with me, you can't come to my birthday party"). Liam is noticeably larger than his classmates—as Ms. Brophy says, "he's a physical presence wherever he is"—and so he often gets his way. But his overly assertive behaviors are hardly conducive to forging lasting friendships.

Everyone is well aware of Liam's friendless status—his teachers, his parents, and certainly Liam himself. One morning in November, Ms. Knowles takes Liam aside. "I've noticed that you're having a hard time making new friends this year," she gently tells him. "I know the other kids want to be your friend. Do you want to be *their* friend as well?" When Liam nods, she asks, "Would it be OK if we talk with the other kids about the problem? Maybe we can all figure out a way to fix it." Liam agrees to her suggestion.

At circle time later in the day, Ms. Knowles says to the children, "You know, everyone in this classroom has something that he or she is working on. For example, I'm trying to grow carrots in my garden. I have to plant them just so, I have to water them two or three times a week, and I have to make sure I keep weeds from growing up around them. Deirdre is learning how to tie her shoes, aren't you, Deirdre?" Deirdre nods. "What are some other things you children are working on?" The children volunteer a variety of works in progress—counting to 100, braiding hair, riding bicycles without training wheels, and so on. Then Ms. Knowles continues, "Well, Liam is working on how to make friends. Friendships are so important, aren't they, boys and girls? Do you have any ideas about how to help him make friends?"

"Don't be a bully," one child suggests. "Ask rather than barge in," says another. "Don't push yourself into line when it's time to go outside," adds a third. The children offer their suggestions with kindness and compassion, and everyone leaves circle time with a sense that something has been accomplished.

Liam's behavior slowly improves after that. He still has moments when he intentionally outruns a classmate to be first in line or thoughtlessly grabs a toy that someone else is using. But when a teacher asks him to choose someone to join him in a short two-person activity, the partner he selects usually goes with him without complaint. And a boy named Miles—a sweet, quiet child who admires Liam's athletic skills—sometimes seeks out his company.

Questions for "The Bully"

1. *Ms. Knowles and Ms. Brophy use a variety of strategies to teach social skills. Which ones do you think might be most effective, and why?*
2. *The teachers occasionally use storybooks to promote discussions about social skills and making friends. For what other areas of social development might children's literature be useful?*
3. *The teachers read the children a letter they claim has been written by their friend Mr. Stone. What are potential advantages of this strategy?*

4.   *Like Liam, aggressive children often alienate their peers. Researchers have identified a variety of reasons why some children are overly aggressive. Which one of the following is **not** a common reason for aggressive behavior in children?*
     a. Low intelligence
     b. Poor perspective-taking ability
     c. Poor social problem-solving skills
     d. Misperception that others have hostile intentions
5.   *What are some possible advantages and disadvantages in Ms. Knowles's approach to helping Liam address his problem in making and keeping friends?*
6.   *Is Ms. Knowles's strategy effective? Why or why not?*

CASE 2
Learning the Ropes

Today is Mindy's first day in Mr. Corbet's kindergarten class. Never before has she been in a room with so many other children her own age. She gets to sit at a blue table with two other girls and two boys. She has her very own chair, which is also blue; it even has her name taped on the back of it. Right now she is coloring a name tag that will be taped to her place at the table, and she is chattering along with the other children who are sitting at her table.

"Hmmm . . . I think I'll color the *M* in pink," Mindy says. "I like pink. It's my favorite color."

Tanya, who is sitting next to her, says, "I think this letter is looking good. Oops, I colored outside the lines on the other one. Oh well . . . what should I color the rest of my letters?"

"This is so easy," Jonathan pipes in. "I did this stuff last year when I went to preschool."

"I wonder if we're going to learn to read today," Grant muses.

The fifth member of the group, Tabitha, scans the room. "When did my mommy leave?" she cries. A bit unnerved, she runs across the room to seek comfort from Mr. Corbet.

Pressing a little too hard, Mindy breaks a green crayon as she begins to color the letter *D* on her name tag. She looks around to see if anyone else has seen what she did; unfortunately, Jonathan has observed the mishap. She walks over to Mr. Corbet so that she can tell him she broke his crayon, but he's preoccupied with Tabitha and so sends her back to her seat. Mindy hides the broken crayon in a box and resumes coloring her name tag.

Jonathan raises his hand straight up in the air. Mindy looks up to see what he is trying to touch, but there's nothing there.

As Mr. Corbet approaches the blue table, Jonathan puts his hand back down. "Well, Jonathan," Mr. Corbet says loudly enough to attract the attention of the entire class, "where did you learn to raise your hand?"

"At preschool," Jonathan replies. He points to Mindy. "That girl broke your crayon."

Mr. Corbet squats down between Mindy and Jonathan. He gently covers Jonathan's hand with his own and curls the boy's pointed finger inward. "It's not nice to point at others or to tattle on them." Jonathan frowns and pulls his hand out of his teacher's grasp.

"What's your new friend's name?" Mr. Corbet asks, looking at Mindy.

Jonathan shrugs. "I don't know."

Mr. Corbet smiles at Mindy and asks, "Would you like to tell him your name?"

Mindy looks at Mr. Corbet, then whispers, "Mindy. I . . . I didn't mean to break your crayon."

"It's OK, Mindy," Mr. Corbet reassures her. "Sometimes that happens with crayons when we press on them too hard. I know you didn't mean to break anything. It's not a big deal. In fact, the more you practice using crayons, the less likely you will be to break them. So then . . . let's find out who else is sitting at the blue table with Mindy and Jonathan. . . . "

After the children have finished coloring their name tags, Mr. Corbet announces, "It's time for recess." Mindy isn't sure what this *recess* thing is, but she can tell by her classmates' excitement that it must be something good.

Mr. Corbet continues, "I'm going to have you line up at the outside door one table at a time. Hmmm . . . I see that the children at the red table are waiting very nicely. So, Red Table, you may be the first ones to line up. Please walk—*walk slowly and quietly*—to the outside door."

Two members of the red table run to be first in line. Ignoring them, Mr. Corbet says, "My, I like how Sam *walks* to the door. Did you see how he *walked,* class? It shows that he's definitely ready to be a kindergartner!"

Mr. Corbet next summons the yellow table. "Wow! Did you notice how every-one in the yellow group *walked?* I can tell that I have a smart class this year."

Mindy squirms in her seat until she hears her teacher call the blue table. When he does so, she makes a concerted effort to walk, not run, to join the line.

Once outside, Mindy stands near Mr. Corbet and watches the other children play on the playground equipment. She has finally concluded that *recess* must be a special place that has swings, monkey bars, tricycles, and other things to play on. A recess is like a park, she thinks, only smaller and without grass or trees. Unlike her kinder-garten classroom, recess is a place where running is allowed. Mindy runs to play with Tanya, her new friend from the blue table.

While the class is outside, Mr. Corbet sometimes blows a loud whistle at particular students. Mindy realizes that the sound of the whistle must not be a good thing, because the children he whistles at have to stop what they're doing and talk with him, and they usually don't look too happy afterwards. Mindy wants to avoid the whistle at all costs, although she's not exactly sure how to go about doing that.

Mindy and Tanya spend most of their play time on the swings. At one point, a girl in a yellow dress pushes Tanya to the ground and then climbs on Tanya's swing as if nothing has happened. Tanya begins to cry, and Mindy looks around for Mr. Corbet. Seeing him close by, she raises her hand and waves it to get his attention.

As Mr. Corbet approaches the girls, Mindy starts to point at the girl in the yellow dress but then immediately closes her fist tight. She nods her head toward the guilty child. "See that girl in the yellow dress?" she asks her teacher. "Well, she pushed Tanya off the swings."

Questions for "Learning the Ropes"

1. The strategies Mr. Corbet uses to teach his students appropriate school behavior are most consistent with which of the following theories?
   a. The theories of Piaget and Erikson
   b. The theories of Bandura and Skinner
   c. The theories of Erikson and Skinner
   d. The theories of Vygotsky and Bandura
2. Children don't always know what is expected of them when they first come to school. What evidence do we see that Mindy lacks knowledge about "how things are done" at school?
3. What strategy does Mr. Corbet use to make his students feel as if they "belong" in their new classroom?
4. At the beginning of the case study, we see Mindy and Tanya talking while they color, yet they don't seem to be listening to each other. How would Piaget explain this event? How would Vygotsky explain it?
5. When Tabitha realizes that her mother has left, she runs to Mr. Corbet for comfort. Such behavior suggests that Tabitha:
   a. Has low self-esteem
   b. Is experiencing disequilibrium
   c. Is in Erikson's trust vs. mistrust stage
   d. Has begun to form an attachment to Mr. Corbet
6. What strategies does Mr. Corbet use to teach his students appropriate behaviors for school and the classroom?
7. Vicarious reinforcement occurs when an individual increases the frequency of a particular response after observing another person being reinforced for that response. What evidence do we see that Mindy has experienced vicarious reinforcement?
8. Vicarious punishment occurs when an individual reduces the frequency of a particular response after observing another person being punished for that response. What evidence do we see that Mindy has experienced vicarious punishment?
9. Children sometimes develop misunderstandings of what certain words mean. What meaning does Mindy construct for the concept **recess**? What existing knowledge does she use in constructing this meaning?

CASE 3
The Paycheck

Five-year-old Rodney, a boy in Ms. Tollefson's kindergarten class, has volunteered to stay after school to help clean up after a messy class art project. As he walks by Ms. Tollefson's desk, he notices her monthly paycheck lying beside her purse.

"Is that a check?" Rodney asks.

"Why, yes, it is," Ms. Tollefson replies, smiling.

"It looks just like the ones my mom and dad bring home all the time."

"Well, that's because your mom and dad both work for the city. I work for the city, too, so I get the same kind of check that they do."

Rodney is shocked. "You have a *job??!!*"

"Yes, of course," says Ms. Tollefson.

"Well, where do you work?"

"I work *here*. My job is teaching you children."

"You get paid for being here? I thought you were just here 'cause you love us."

"Well, I do love all of you. But I also get paid to work, just like your mom and dad get paid to work. Just like your parents, I need money to pay for things like food, medicine, and clothes."

"No you don't. Teachers don't need money. When you're in this building you always get food from the cafeteria where we get our morning snacks. And you have clothes every day 'cause you wear them. All you have to do is go over to that closet"—Rodney points to a small closet in the back of the room—"and grab a new outfit."

"Rodney, I keep my clothes at home just like you do."

"You have a home? I didn't know teachers left the building."

"You thought I *slept* here?"

"Well, actually I never thought about you sleeping. I just thought that this was your home."

"No. I sleep—live, actually—in a house just like you do. As a matter of fact, my house is just a few blocks from yours. You may even show up at my doorstep when you go trick-or-treating for Halloween tomorrow night."

"I think you're teasing me, Ms. Tollefson. Teachers don't live in houses. Teachers belong at school."

"Can't I be other things besides a teacher, Rodney? For example, did you know that I go skiing every weekend in the winter? So I'm a skier as well as a teacher. See, here's a picture of me skiing at Winter Park."

"You can't fool me, Ms. Tollefson," Rodney responds cheerfully as he skips out the door. "I know you're just a teacher."

"Happy Halloween!" yells Ms. Tollefson.

Rodney pokes his head back inside the classroom. "I knew it! You were trying to trick me 'cause it's Halloween!" Laughing, he runs down the hall before his teacher can reply.

Questions for "The Paycheck"

1. Ms. Tollefson explains to Rodney why her paycheck looks similar to the checks his parents bring home. From the perspective of Vygotskian theorists, her explanation is a good example of which one of the following?
   a. Discovery learning
   b. Direct instruction
   c. Disequilibrium in action
   d. A mediated learning experience
2. From the perspective of Piaget's theory, what evidence of preoperational reasoning does Rodney exhibit?
3. How might we explain Rodney's thinking from an information-processing perspective?
4. Psychologists have offered a variety of reasons as to why children sometimes have naive ideas about the world. Rodney clearly has a very naive view of what a **teacher** is. Three of the following factors may have contributed to his misconception in this situation. Which one is **least** likely to have done so?
   a. Children are apt to draw conclusions based on how things appear to be.
   b. Common expressions in language sometimes misrepresent the true nature of physical events.
   c. Many children have a very limited knowledge base to use in elaborating on their observations and experiences.
   d. Children may perpetuate their misbeliefs by disregarding information that is inconsistent with those beliefs.
5. In what way is the conversation between Ms. Tollefson and Rodney most likely to promote Rodney's social-emotional development?
   a. It should enhance Rodney's sense of self.
   b. It should encourage Rodney to act more prosocially.
   c. It should enhance Rodney's perspective-taking ability.
   d. It should facilitate Rodney's attachment to his teacher.

CASE 4
The Goldfish

As the final school bell rings, most of the students in Ms. Bowman's first-grade class gather their belongings and hurry out the door. But Amy convinces her friend Lucy to linger for a few minutes while she checks on Ringo, the class's pet goldfish. As this week's "animal keeper" for the class, Amy has noticed that Ringo hasn't eaten any of his food for the past 2 days. In fact, all he does now is lie sideways on the surface of the water; he doesn't try to swim away when she touches him. With her friend looking over her shoulder, Amy tries to give the fish a slight push toward a few flakes of food.

"He must be sleeping," she says. "Usually all I have to do is swish the water around to make him swim. He's acting really weird. Maybe he's *forgotten* how to eat and swim."

Lucy inspects the fish and then looks back at her friend and says, "I don't know, Amy. He's been sleeping an awful long time. He's not eating either. I'll get Ms. Bowman, and maybe she can fix him."

Lucy hurries over to her teacher and grabs her by the hand. "Something's wrong," Amy declares as Lucy and Ms. Bowman approach the fish bowl. "He's not moving. He hasn't eaten for a long time."

When Ms. Bowman looks in the bowl, she realizes that Ringo has died. She delicately explains the situation and then wraps the fish in a paper towel. She assures the girls that she will give Ringo a proper burial as soon as she gets home.

Amy looks puzzled. "But . . . but . . . when my grandpa died last summer, he went away to heaven and didn't come back. Ringo's still here. If he's dead, he should be going to heaven."

"Do you want Ringo to go to heaven?" Amy nods, and Ms. Bowman smiles. "Well, then, I bet he'll go there just as soon as he possibly can."

As the two girls walk home, Lucy poses a question: "Do you have to eat in heaven?"

"I don't know," Amy responds. "I suppose so, or else you'd be hungry all the time."

"Oh, that makes sense." Lucy pauses for a moment and then asks, "Well, do you have to go potty in heaven?"

Amy rolls her eyes, indignantly puts her hands on her hips, and replies, "Of course not, silly! You know our mommies and Ms. Bowman make us go potty before we go *anywhere!*"

"Oh, yeah, I forgot," laughs Lucy.

Questions for "The Goldfish"

1. *Amy's previous experience with her grandfather's death led her to believe that people and other living creatures "go away" when they die, yet the fish is still in the fish bowl. From Piaget's perspective, this situation is likely to:*
   a. *Increase Amy's egocentrism*
   b. *Create disequilibrium for Amy*
   c. *Promote concrete operational thinking*
   d. *Be beyond Amy's zone of proximal development*
2. *Piaget described the preoperational stage as being characterized by egocentric thinking. Identify a possible instance of egocentrism in the case.*
3. *How might one interpret Amy's conclusions about eating and "going potty" from an information-processing perspective of cognitive development?*
4. *How might a Vygotskian theorist suggest Ms. Bowman address the death of the class pet?*
5. *How might taking care of pets in the classroom promote students' cognitive development? Their social-emotional development?*
6. *To what extent should Ms. Bowman have discussed the concepts of death and heaven with the entire class?*

CASE 5
Haley and Meredith

I teach first grade at a small private school just outside of New York City. Most of the children who attend the school come from very wealthy families; many have full-time nannies and one or more live-in servants at home. A lot of my kids have "issues." It's clear that money doesn't necessarily solve life's problems.

Take Haley, for instance. She's terribly afraid of men. She gets hysterical if a strange man walks into the classroom. And she won't go to my class's weekly violin lesson because the school's violin teacher is male.

Another thing about Haley is that she lives in the shadow of her older sister, Heidi, who's a third grader at our school. Mom dresses the two girls alike each day. She thinks Heidi is perfect and often tells Haley to "be more like your sister." When Haley gets upset, she asks if she can go see Heidi, and when Heidi stays home sick, Haley cries all day. As you can see, the sisters are very close. Too close, in fact. When I ask my students to write about themselves, Haley usually writes about Heidi instead. And once when I asked the kids to draw self-portraits, Haley drew a picture of Heidi!

Haley has one good friend in class and seems lost if this friend isn't there. Her name is Meredith, and she often carpools with Haley and Heidi. She's very smart. She's also very aggressive. One day she pushed a girl down the stairs. Another time she shoved a chair leg into a boy's foot. Haley looks to Meredith for clues about how to behave and obeys Meredith's every command, partly because Meredith pinches or punches her if she doesn't. Meredith treats *her own mother* this way. One day Meredith wanted to come to school dressed like Britney Spears—you know, with a miniskirt and a tight, skimpy top that showed her navel. Mom tried to discourage the outfit, but Meredith hit her, and so we had "Britney" in class that day.

No one except me ever holds Meredith accountable for her behavior. At home she constantly has servants and her nanny waiting on her while her mother goes shopping or works out at the gym. Here's a 6-year-old who doesn't know how to dress herself! She can't even zip up her jacket or tie her shoes.

Questions for "Haley and Meredith"

1. *Perhaps Haley's fear of men is the result of previous bad experiences (possibly including child abuse) with one or two men. If so, which of the following concepts from learning theory can probably best explain Haley's fear of men?*
    a. Working memory and elaboration
    b. Operant conditioning and shaping

We thank an anonymous colleague for providing this case study.

      c. *Modeling and reciprocal causation*

      d. *Classical conditioning and generalization*

2. *What concerns should you have about Haley's sense of self?*

3. *If you were to explain Meredith's aggressive behaviors from the perspective of* **operant conditioning,** *which one of the following statements would be most appropriate?*

      a. *Meredith is biologically predisposed to aggressive behavior.*

      b. *Meredith has been reinforced for acting aggressively in the past.*

      c. *Meredith has often seen important people in her life act aggressively toward others.*

      d. *Meredith perceives other people's misdeeds as being intentional actions to hurt her in some way.*

4. *What strategies might a teacher use in working with Haley?*

5. *What strategies might a teacher use in working with Meredith?*

CASE 6
Houses and Boats

While waiting for a visit from the local fire chief, Mr. Rodriguez asks his third graders to draw floor plans of their homes—as he puts it, to "draw what a bird would see if the roof were missing." Once the fire chief arrives, the children will use red colored markers to create several fire exit routes in their floor plans.

As the children work at tables of four students each, Mr. Rodriguez walks around the room to oversee their efforts. He notices that Jenny is copying Tian's floor plan on her own paper.

"Jenny, do you live in the same house as Tian?" he asks her.

"No."

"Then why are you copying his drawing?"

"Because I don't know how to draw things on my own."

"Of course you do. I'm asking you to draw *your* house, not just any old house."

"I can't."

"Jenny, I was your kindergarten teacher. I remember that you used to draw *lovely* pictures."

"Maybe, but I don't remember how to draw houses anymore."

"You don't *remember* how to draw them?"

"That's right. I can't do it by myself, so you'll have to show me how."

"Well, I can at least help you get started. How many stories does your house have?"

"Two."

"OK, let's start with the first floor. How many rooms are there on the first floor of your house?"

"Um . . . let's see . . . there's the living room and the dining room and the kitchen and the bathroom. That's four."

"Is there also a hallway with stairs going up to the second floor?"

"Yes."

"OK. Now what shape is your house? What shape would it be if a bird were looking down at it?"

"A rectangle, I guess."

"So start by drawing a rectangle on your paper. Good, now why don't you show me where the front door is in this rectangle house of yours, and then we can talk about where each room should go and where we should put the stairs . . . "

During the fire chief's visit, Ms. Piesman, the art teacher, arrives carrying a stack of watercolor paintings. "Say, your students did a wonderful job painting these boats," she tells Mr. Rodriguez. "I thought I'd hang them up in the hallway. Would that be all right with you?"

"Sounds like a good idea. If you have time now, I can help you hang them."

"Thanks, I'd appreciate that."

As the two teachers begin hanging the paintings in the hallway on both sides of the classroom door, Mr. Rodriguez comments, "This is the first time all year that I've had a chance to see any of the children's art work." He pauses to stare at the paintings. "Hey! All of these boats look the same."

"Of course."

"I mean, everyone used the exact same proportions, the same colors, the same . . . everything!"

"Yes," Ms. Piesman responds proudly. "It took me awhile, but I finally got everyone to think on the same wavelength."

Questions for "Houses and Boats"

1. From Erik Erikson's perspective, in what stage of development should Jenny be?
2. Why might Jenny be having trouble creating her floor plan?
3. When Mr. Rodriguez helps Jenny with her picture, he asks her a series of questions that guide her initial steps. Which one of the following theoretical concepts best describes what Mr. Rodriguez is doing?
    a. Behaviorist theory's concept of **shaping**
    b. Vygotskian theory's concept of **scaffolding**
    c. Piagetian theory's concept of **assimilation**
    d. Social learning theory's concept of **modeling**
4. Is it wise for Ms. Piesman to insist that the children all make their boats in the same way? Why or why not?
5. What strategies might Ms. Piesman use to encourage creativity in her art classes?

CASE 7
The Art Box

Except for Lilly, who has suddenly lost her art box, all of Mr. King's third graders are in line and ready to go to Ms. Wilson's art class. Lilly checks her backpack but finds it empty. She doesn't remember taking her art supplies home, but she must have—because her markers, scissors, colored pencils, and glue are nowhere to be found. Finally giving up, Lilly runs to join her friends at the end of the line.

After she and her father have looked everywhere at home yet still found no sign of the art box, Lilly tells Mr. King that her art supplies are missing. Mr. King explains the situation to the class, suggests that maybe someone accidentally picked up the wrong box, and asks that all of the children look carefully inside their desks. None of the children mentions finding either the box or its contents.

Over the weekend, Lilly and her father go shopping to replace the supplies she has lost. After arriving back home, Lilly's father painstakingly writes "Lilly" on each new item with a black permanent marker. Yet by Thursday of the following week, Lilly cannot find the crayons and bottle of glue her father has recently purchased. She assures Mr. King that she has kept her supplies in her art box and that the box has remained in her desk the entire week. Mr. King doesn't know what to make of the situation but is beginning to think that Lilly is either very forgetful or very disorganized. And when Lilly's father has to buy yet another round of art supplies for his daughter, he is not at all pleased.

A few weeks later, Lilly sees Anne using a bottle of glue with the name "Lilly" written on it. Lilly confronts her classmate: "Where did you get that glue?"

"My mom bought it for me," Anne replies.

"Then how come it has my name written on it?" Lilly asks.

"'Cause my sister's name is Lilly, and we share everything."

"I don't believe you. I'm telling the teacher."

After listening to Lilly's complaint, Mr. King confronts Anne, asking, "Honey, where did you get that bottle of glue?"

"My mom gave it to me and my sister Lilly."

"Are you sure?" asks Mr. King.

"Yes," Anne replies. "My mom always gives me things, 'cause she loves me."

"I see." Mr. King pauses, then adds, "I think it's time the two of you get back to work."

Suspecting that Anne is being dishonest, Mr. King sifts through the contents of her desk while the class is at recess. He finds two art boxes with Lilly's name on them, several boxes of crayons marked with various children's initials, an assortment of glue bottles, and a Colorado Rockies pen in the shape of a baseball bat that he's pretty sure belongs to Owen. Leaving these items where he's found them, Mr. King calls Anne's parents and requests a conference immediately after school. Just before the final bell, Mr. King informs Anne that her parents are coming to pick her up and asks her to stay in her seat until they arrive.

"What's this about?" says Anne's father, Mr. Walker, as he ignores Mr. King's outstretched hand. "I had to cancel several clients at the office to come to this meeting."

"I'm delighted to finally meet you both," Mr. King responds. "I'm also grateful that you were able to come on such short notice. Perhaps we can sit at the reading table over here. I apologize for the size of the chairs. They're meant for 8-year-olds rather than adults, I'm afraid."

Once Anne and her parents have taken their seats at the table, Mr. King continues, "This may seem like a strange question, but I would like to know if you have another daughter—one named Lilly."

"Lilly?" Mrs. Walker seems puzzled. "No, Anne is our only child."

"You called me away from the office to ask if we have another *daughter?*" Mr. Walker asks angrily.

Mr. King tries to keep his composure. "Well, over the past few weeks, a number of my students have found items missing from their desks. This afternoon I found many of the items in Anne's desk." He pauses to see if either Anne or one of her parents has anything to say at this point, but all three are silent. He continues, "I can't seem to get a straight answer from Anne as to how other children's things have ended up in her desk. I was hoping that maybe . . . if we could get together to talk about it . . . we could figure out what's going on."

Mr. Walker stands up, clearly uncomfortable with Mr. King's implied accusation. He turns to his daughter and says, "OK, Anne, let's go take a look at your desk." Anne leads the way, and the three adults follow. When Anne opens her desk, several items marked "Lilly" are lying in plain sight.

Mr. Walker is obviously taken aback at the discovery. "So how'd these things get in your desk, Anne?" he asks.

"Kids gave them to me so I'd be their friend," Anne replies tentatively as she looks down at the floor.

Mr. Walker looks at Mr. King and says, "There you have it. My daughter knows I expect her to obey rules like not stealing and not lying. Don't you, Anne?" When Anne nods in agreement, he continues, "If she says the other kids gave them to her, then they *gave* them to her."

Mr. King looks Anne directly in the eye. "Anne, didn't you tell me that these things belonged to your sister Lilly?"

"Like my wife said earlier, Anne doesn't have a sister Lilly!" Mr. Walker barks.

Mr. King is firm. "Tell your parents what you told me earlier, Anne."

"I said my *friend* Lilly gave me her art boxes and some of her crayons and glue. You just didn't listen, Mr. King."

"Hmmm . . . ," Mr. King responds pensively, "I think . . . "

Mr. Walker rudely interrupts: "She says she didn't take that stuff. It's not her fault that she's so popular. She obeys me at home—no stealing and no lying. Why should she be different in school? Sure, sometimes she's a little brat, but what kid isn't?" Mr. Walker speaks as if Anne isn't even in the room.

Mrs. Walker reaches out and pulls her daughter toward her in a protective embrace. "She's just a little girl. What if she did take that stuff?"

"She didn't!" screams Mr. Walker.

"It's just some crayons and pencils. Altogether it can't be worth more than five dollars," Mrs. Walker suggests. "Why should she be punished if none of the items was destroyed?"

"I'm afraid that you both are missing the point here," Mr. King responds. "Lilly, one of the other children in my class, has had to replace her art supplies twice now because they've suddenly disappeared, and then today I find her possessions in Anne's desk."

"How do you know Lilly didn't just give these things to Anne?!" demands Mr. Walker.

"Well, for one thing, several weeks ago Lilly told me that her art box was missing. It seems unlikely she would tell me that if she knew she had given the box to Anne."

"So you're taking *her* word over my daughter's?" Mr. Walker retorts. "I expect Anne to follow my rules, and I think she does. How do we know that Lilly isn't lying? Where are *her* parents? Why isn't she being called on the carpet the way Anne is right now?"

"But look at the evidence in her desk. The items are clearly labeled with other children's names. Anne can't possibly be completely innocent . . . "

"Leave my daughter out of this!" Mr. Walker screams. "I expect you to set an example for my child. You should have had all the facts before you went accusing someone. Come on, Anne, let's go home. Mr. King needs to think about what he has done!"

Mr. King watches in total frustration as the Walkers leave his classroom in a huff.

Note: Throughout her school career, Anne continued to take no responsibility for her actions, nor were her parents ever willing to face up to their daughter's wrongdoings.

Questions for "The Art Box"

1. *From the perspective of Kohlberg's theory of moral development, how might you best interpret Anne's behavior?*
   a. *She is at Kohlberg's conventional level, believing that "might makes right."*
   b. *She is at Kohlberg's postconventional level, believing that rules apply to others but not to her.*

    c. *She is at Kohlberg's preconventional level, believing that any behavior that goes unpunished is acceptable.*

    d. *She is at Kohlberg's "social contract" stage, believing that her own needs take precedence over those of others.*

2. *Why do you think Anne stole the items?*

3. *Because Anne has essentially been reinforced for stealing (i.e., she has obtained desirable items without negative repercussions), she is apt to steal again. As the teacher, what might you do to prevent other thefts from occurring in this classroom?*

4. *Developmental researchers have described several different parenting styles (authoritative, authoritarian, permissive, uninvolved) that parents use in raising their children. What type of parenting style does Mr. Walker exhibit?*

5. *What type of parenting style does Mrs. Walker exhibit?*

6. *Mr. King makes a common mistake: His first contact with the Walkers is a negative one. As a teacher, how might you initiate more positive initial contacts with students' parents?*

7. *What things might Mr. King have done to make the parent conference go more smoothly?*

8. *Describe at least three different strategies Mr. King might use to help Anne acquire and abide by internal standards for moral behavior—in other words, to promote Anne's moral development.*

CASE 8
The Emergency Telephone Call

Near the end of the school day, Mr. Wadsworth has an emergency telephone call and finds that he must leave his fifth-grade class temporarily unattended. He puts Sandy, a particularly trustworthy student, in charge, asking her to keep the other students in their seats and on task. He also asks her to report any misbehaviors to him upon his return.

After listening to their teacher's footsteps grow fainter and fainter as he walks down the hall, many of the children begin talking and joking with one another. The longer Mr. Wadsworth is gone, the louder the volume of their chatter becomes. "Oh, *great!*" thinks Sandy. "Do I report *all* of them?"

Suzanne, a popular girl whom Sandy admires, shouts, "Hey, let's play some tricks on Mr. Wadsworth!" She runs up to her teacher's desk, grabs several tacks from the desk drawer, and strategically scatters them on Mr. Wadsworth's chair at the reading table. Sandy approaches her friend and whispers, "Suzanne, you need to put those tacks back. You know this is wrong. Mr. Wadsworth might hurt himself."

"Lighten up, Sandy. Besides, he'll never know who did it, will he?"

"It's wrong . . . "

"It's only wrong if you get *caught,* Sandy."

Suzanne sees a bottle of glue on Mr. Wadsworth's desk. Ignoring Sandy's pleas to stop, she takes several of the textbooks lying on Mr. Wadsworth's desk and glues some of the pages together. Then, hiding the empty glue bottle in her desk, Suzanne looks around to see if any of the other children have noticed what she has done, but they seem to be wrapped up in off-task activities of their own.

After pausing to think about additional pranks she can play, Suzanne puts the class hamster, George, in the bottom file drawer of her teacher's desk. As an afterthought, she pours some water in a plastic cup and places it in the drawer along with the hamster.

"Suzanne, what you're doing isn't nice to George, to Mr. Wadsworth, or to me. Mr. Wadsworth is going to be really angry at me for letting you do these things. I know you think you're being funny, but you're not!"

"Sandy, I thought we were friends."

"We are."

"Friends trust one another and share secrets. Anyway, there won't be a problem if I don't get caught."

"Well, yeah, but I don't like keeping this kind of secret. Mr. Wadsworth trusts me. Besides, he'll probably punish the whole class for what you've done!"

Ignoring Sandy, Suzanne grabs red and black permanent markers and proceeds to draw pictures of Mr. Wadsworth on the dry eraser board hanging on the wall. The other students grow quiet as they watch Suzanne draw her pictures. Sandy lays her head on her desk in hopeless resignation.

"Suzanne, those are permanent markers," Dillon calls out. "You won't be able to erase that stuff."

"Oh, come on, Wadsworth can get rid of them," Suzanne retorts. "All he has to do is use rubbing alcohol and the ink will come right off."

"Why should *he* clean up *your* mess?" Molly asks indignantly.

"Man, you're really gonna get in trouble!" Blake warns.

Suzanne turns and glares at her classmates. "I won't get in trouble unless there's a 'narc' in here."

The others look to Sandy for help, but she still has her head on her desk. When the final bell rings and Mr. Wadsworth has still not returned to his classroom, the children slowly gather their things and depart for home.

Suzanne leaves the uncapped markers on the eraser board shelf and gathers her belongings. "Do you want to walk home together?" she asks Sandy.

"No, I . . . uh . . . have to stay after school for choir."

"Oh, I see. You're going to 'narc' on me, aren't you?"

"Uh, no, probably not . . . no, of course not. But I think you should tell Mr. Wadsworth what you've done."

"Oh, come on, Sandy. It was all just a joke."

"Well, it wasn't a very funny one."

After Suzanne leaves, Sandy walks to the office and asks Ms. Leary, the school secretary, for some rubbing alcohol.

"Why do you need it?" Ms. Leary asks her.

"Uh. . . well, you see . . . uh . . . someone accidentally got some permanent marker on the erasable marker board. I was going to clean it off for Mr. Wadsworth." Sandy looks down at her feet.

"Honey, you don't have to worry about it," Ms. Leary tells her. "Mr. Schroeder, the custodian, will clean it up."

"That's OK, I don't mind. I . . . uh . . . kinda like cleaning the boards."

"No, that's Mr. Schroeder's job. You run on home."

Sandy returns to her classroom to see if she can find Mr. Wadsworth. She should have been home a half hour ago. "Great," she thinks, "now Mom is going to be mad at me too."

Mr. Wadsworth walks into the room. When he sees Sandy he says, "There you are! Your mother just called. She's very worried about you. Why are you still here?"

Before she can respond, Mr. Wadsworth sees the board. "What the heck . . . who wrote on the board with permanent markers?"

Sandy bursts into tears. "I tried to make them behave. Really I did!"

"The *whole class* did this?"

"No, just someone . . . just one person. But no one did anything about it, so I didn't either."

Mr. Wadsworth stoops down to Sandy's level, looks her straight in the eye, and asks, "Who did this, Sandy?"

She shrugs her shoulders.

"If you don't tell me who was responsible for this mess, then you will have to be the one to clean it up."

Sandy stares at the floor.

Mr. Wadsworth leaves the room, returning shortly with a bottle of clear liquid. He hands the bottle to Sandy, saying, "I expected better of you, Sandy. Maybe cleaning the marker board will refresh your memory. By the way, your mother is on her way over."

While Sandy cleans the board, Mr. Wadsworth sits at his desk to grade papers. He opens the bottom drawer to look for his grading book, only to find the class hamster scampering about and water sloshing from one side of the drawer to the other. He sees, too, that all the teaching materials he keeps in that drawer have been chewed by the hamster and saturated with water.

Mr. Wadsworth explodes. "Sandy, George is in my desk! He's ruined everything. Who did this? Tell me *now!*"

Sandy replies so quietly that Mr. Wadsworth can barely hear her. "She did more stuff, too. She ruined some of your books. She . . . um . . . glued a bunch of pages together."

Gathering his composure, Mr. Wadsworth repeats his question. "Who did this, Sandy?"

"Suzanne. She said I'd be a 'narc' if I told. Please don't tell her I told you, Mr. Wadsworth. *Please!*"

Note: Suzanne was officially charged with a misdemeanor: She was suspended 3 days for willful destruction of school property. The municipal court judge mandated that before she could return to school, her parents would have to reimburse the school district for the damages she had caused. Several years after the incident, Suzanne and Sandy still weren't speaking to each other.

Questions for "The Emergency Telephone Call"

1. *Is it appropriate for Mr. Wadsworth to put Sandy in charge of the class during his absence? Why or why not?*
2. *From Kohlberg's perspective, in what stage of moral development is each of the girls?*
3. *Should the entire class be punished for allowing Suzanne to vandalize the classroom? Why or why not?*
4. *Should Sandy be punished for failing to provide adequate supervision? Why or why not?*
5. *What functions do friendships, like that of Sandy and Suzanne, serve for children and adolescents? With these functions in mind, explain why Sandy is torn about whether to be truthful with Mr. Wadsworth.*

6.   *Three of the following are potentially productive strategies that Mr. Wadsworth might use in discussing Suzanne's inappropriate behaviors with her parents. Which strategy is **least** likely to be effective?*
   a. *Acknowledge that raising children can often be a challenging task.*
   b. *Focus the discussion exclusively on Suzanne's inappropriate behavior.*
   c. *Seek information that might provide insights into why Suzanne behaved as she did.*
   d. *Try to get consensus about how the misbehavior will be addressed at school and at home.*

CASE 9
Friends

Tanner and Ethan have been Jared's closest friends since preschool. The three boys have always had much in common; over the years, they've had similar interests—first Legos, then lizards, and eventually model trains. They belonged to the same Cub Scout troop, and they've always made sure they were on the same team in the city baseball and basketball leagues. They've even dressed alike, wearing T-shirts, jeans, high-top sneakers, and Atlanta Braves baseball caps. At their small neighborhood school, they've always been in the same class.

But now that they're in junior high school, things seem to be different. Although Jared and Ethan have lockers next to each other, the three boys have been assigned to different homerooms and different classes, and each one eats during a different lunch period, so they hardly ever see one another during the school day. Furthermore, Tanner and Ethan don't seem to be the same guys they used to be. Tanner started wearing an earring the week after school began. His clothes are different, too. His baggy pants hang down low on his hips, and his shirts are always so large that they reach almost to his knees. He's usually so interested in flirting with girls in the hallway or riding his new skateboard with the other "skaters" in the school parking lot that he has little time for Jared.

Ethan has changed, too, although in different ways than Tanner has. For example, he's about 6 inches taller than he was last year. His voice has grown deep like his dad's. He's become a real "neatnik," with his hair carefully combed and his designer shirts tucked carefully inside his well-pressed pants. He's joined the soccer team and stays after school every day for 2 hours of soccer practice. Like Tanner, Ethan seems to have little interest in maintaining his friendship with Jared.

Thinking that he would be too busy playing football after school with his friends, Jared didn't sign up for any of the extracurricular activities at his new school. So he comes home right after school each day and retreats to the basement to play with his model trains.

"Gosh, Jared, I haven't seen Ethan and Tanner over here for quite some time," his mother comments one day. "Don't you ever see them at school?"

"Not really, Mom," Jared replies. "And they're usually too busy when I ask them to come over."

"Well, you know, I ran into Ethan's mother at the grocery store the other day, and she said that Ethan made lots of new friends when he joined the soccer team. Maybe you should think about joining one of the teams or clubs at school too. What about the swimming team, or the Spanish club, or maybe the school band?"

As luck would have it, Jared sees announcements for school band tryouts posted around the school building the following day. Having taken a few trumpet lessons when he was in fourth grade, Jared thinks that playing trumpet in the band might be fun. When he gets home that afternoon, he pulls his trumpet out of his closet and begins to practice. "It's coming back to me," he happily discovers.

Questions for "Friends"

1. *The transition to middle school or junior high school is often an unsettling time for students because many changes seem to occur almost simultaneously. What specific changes do we see at this point in time?*
2. *If you were a junior high school teacher, what strategies might you use to make new students feel more comfortable and secure?*
3. *In Erik Erikson's view, in which stage of psychosocial development are the three boys likely to be?*
    a. Initiative vs. guilt
    b. Intimacy vs. isolation
    c. Industry vs. inferiority
    d. Identity vs. role confusion
4. *Explain Jared's newly found interest in extracurricular activities using the concept of* **vicarious reinforcement.**
5. *Identify various benefits that participation in extracurricular activities might have for young adolescents.*

CASE 10
Alabama

Until last week, Tom attended a small school in Alabama at which almost everyone, teachers and students alike, were people he'd known for years. But now that his family has moved to Indiana, he has enrolled at a junior high school with more than 300 students in just the seventh and eighth grades alone. Naturally, he doesn't know a soul.

On the first day at his new school, Tom is dumbfounded by the other students' language. They talk a lot faster than the people in Alabama do, and no one addresses teachers as "ma'am" or "sir." The students dress differently, too. Most of them wear over-sized T-shirts and ripped jeans, and some of the boys wear their pants so low on their hips that their boxer shorts show. Amazingly, the teachers don't seem to mind how his peers are dressed. Back in Alabama, Tom would have been sent home for such attire.

In his first-period English class, Tom notices several of his classmates snickering at his white shirt, necktie, and khaki pants. One of them, a boy named Sam, asks him, "Hey, man, where you from?"

"Alabama," Tom replies. "This is my first day here."

"Don't you wear jeans in Allaaabaaamma?" Sam inquires, stretching out the word *Alabama* to mimic Tom's southern drawl.

"Of course we wear jeans," Tom responds. "But I wouldn't dream of coming to school with holes in my pants or with my underwear showing."

Sam winks at the small group of girls who are watching the interaction. "I bet you wouldn't, Allaaabaaamma." Tom hears the girls snicker and feels his face turn red. He buries his head in the textbook his teacher has just given him.

Tom stays after school to try out for the boys' spring track team, a team on which he excelled back in Alabama. Sam and several of the other boys in his English class are at the tryouts as well. Tom is the only one wearing a bright red Lycra jogging suit. Everyone else is wearing blue cotton sweat pants and white T-shirts. Tom realizes that blue and white must be the school colors.

"What's the matter, Alabama, don't they have sweat pants where you come from?" Sam jeers. "Who do you think you are—Michael Jordan? Say, Allaaabaaamma, I sure hope you don't run as slow as you talk."

Several of the other boys are trembling with laughter. Tom says nothing, but he grits his teeth and clenches his fists in anger as he walks over to the bleachers to sit near the track coach, Mr. Davis. He wishes his family had never moved to Indiana. The students are so strange here, and he feels completely out of place.

"OK, gentlemen, let's get started," Coach Davis calls out. As all the boys gather around him, he continues, "There are more than 60 of you here today. I'm very pleased that so many of you have come out. Unfortunately, I have only 24 spots on the team, so we'll have to see which of you are the fastest. I'm going to divide you into groups of three and have you race around the track. We'll see who's the fastest in each group."

Tom finds himself in the same group as Sam and a boy named Eddie, who's in his science class. As the three boys run around the track, they are initially neck and neck. But suddenly Eddie trips, knocking Sam, and the two boys fall. Tom looks back and sees both Sam and Eddie lying on the track. Sam seems to have gotten a nasty gash on his knee. Tom immediately turns around and trots over to Sam, grabs his hand, and helps him get up.

Coach Davis approaches the threesome to make sure everyone is all right. "It looks like we'll have to run this race again," Tom tells him.

"Hey, Alabama," Sam says (not mocking Tom this time), "why didn't you finish the race? You could easily have won it."

"When I win, I want to know it's a *true* win."

A short time later, Sam and Eddie both outrun Tom, and Tom is eliminated from further consideration. Sam offers his hand to Tom. "Good try, Alabama. Thanks for letting me have another go at it." Tom shakes Sam's hand and smiles, trying to hide his disappointment about not making the team.

The following morning, some of the boys in Tom's English class are reveling in their success at making the track team. In an attempt to draw attention to themselves, a few start to pick on Tom.

"Hey, Alabama, don't you know your way around a track?" Cory taunts. "Or maybe a circle's just too much for you!"

"Did your mommy comfort you when she found out you're a loser, Alabama?" Greg adds.

"Wow, Alabama, you're wearing your shirt untucked today," Mick observes. "Aren't *you* a cool dude!"

"Why don't you guys just leave Alabama alone?" Sam suggests, obviously annoyed.

"What's with you, Sam?" Cory asks him. "Maybe you're from Alabama, too, and you're just hiding your accent."

"No, I'm not from Alabama!" Sam exclaims. He lowers his voice and continues, "Anyway, what if I was? Nothing's wrong with comin' from there."

At the end of class, Sam slips Tom a note. It reads: "There's a computer club meeting tonight. None of these boys are in it. Call me."

Note: At Tom's school in Alabama, there had been no competition for extracurricular activities; the school was so small that clubs and sports teams typically accepted anyone who wanted to join them. Tom clearly felt uncomfortable in the competitive atmosphere of his new school. Aside from the computer club, he didn't participate in extracurricular activities.

Questions for "Alabama"

1. *Characterize Tom's initial reaction to his new school.*
2. *The differing expectations between Tom's Alabama school (which expected formal dress and speech) and Tom's new school (at which standards for dress and speech are more relaxed) illustrate which one of the following phenomena?*
   a. Assimilation
   b. Self-handicapping
   c. Cultural mismatch
   d. Multicultural education
3. *How successfully does Tom adjust to the culture of his new school?*
4. *It is not unusual for students at this age to make jokes at someone else's expense. As a teacher, what should you do if you hear such teasing in your classroom?*
5. *Tom stops during the race to help Sam and Eddie, who have both fallen. When questioned about his behavior, Tom replies, "When I win, I want to know it's a* **true** *win." Lawrence Kohlberg would most likely categorize Tom's reasoning as falling within which stage of moral development?*
   a. Stage 1: Punishment-avoidance and obedience
   b. Stage 2: Exchange of favors
   c. Stage 3: Good boy/good girl
   d. Stage 4: Law and order
6. *As a teacher, how might you help Tom make friends at his new school?*
7. *Many middle schools and junior high schools have a "no cuts" policy regarding extracurricular activities; in other words, teams and clubs accept anyone who wants to join them. Is this a good idea? Why or why not?*

CASE 11
Studying French

Every Thursday night of her freshman year in high school, Karen studies for the quiz she knows she will have in her French I class the following morning. She begins her study sessions by preparing flash cards for the week's vocabulary words, writing each new word on one side of an index card and then copying the word's definition onto the flip side. After completing her flash cards, Karen locks herself in her room, turns on the radio, then repeats each word and its definition five times to herself. Unfortunately, her strategy doesn't seem to be working very well. Although she's getting A's and B's in her other classes, the highest score she's earned in French I is 72%—a C–.

In May, as she and her friends are signing up for next year's classes, Karen is trying to decide whether or not to take a second year of French. She is well aware that the college she wants to attend requires its students to have at least 2 years of a foreign language. And her two best friends, Dawnece and Claire, are urging her to take Mr. Lanier's third-hour French II class with them. Dawnece reminds her that the French club is going to Paris the following summer. "Besides," Dawnece says, "Mr. Lanier is so *cute!*"

Karen blushes and grins sheepishly. "Oh, what the heck! I can't possibly do any worse in French II than I've been doing in French I."

The following September, Karen begins to panic as the first test approaches in her French II class. "No matter how hard I try, I'm just no good at French," she thinks. "Will Dawnece think I'm stupid if I ask her to study with me? Claire probably doesn't study at all. She's lucky; her parents are both French, so she was *born* knowing this stuff."

Karen brings up the subject at lunch. "You know, our first French test is tomorrow."

"Yeah, what a pain," Dawnece replies. "I hate studying."

"Me, too," Claire adds.

"Uh . . . yeah." Karen pauses for a moment. "Say, I was wondering if . . . um . . . Dawnece, I thought maybe we could study together." She nervously scrutinizes Dawnece's facial expression, wondering if her friend will think she's crazy for asking.

But Dawnece apparently doesn't think she's crazy at all. "Hey, sure! Claire and I are going to study at my house at 6:30 tonight. Come join us."

Karen seems quite surprised. "You and *Claire?* Claire, you *study* for your French tests?"

Claire laughs. "Of course!"

"But your parents are *French!*"

"My mom moved to the United States when she was 3, and my dad moved here when he was a teenager. You know perfectly well that both my parents speak English at home. My mom says she doesn't even *remember* any French. Besides, don't *you* study for your *English* tests?"

"Well, yeah, I *guess* so, but . . . "

"Like, it's the same thing!"

To prepare for her study session with Dawnece and Claire, Karen makes flash cards for all the vocabulary words the class has studied so far. She wonders whether her friends have completed their cards already or will instead make them while they study. She spends an hour or so repeating the words and definitions on her flash cards and then arrives at Dawnece's door around 6:45.

"We started without you," Dawnece tells her. "I hope you don't mind."

When Karen notices that neither girl has any flash cards in front of her, she keeps her own cards hidden in her backpack. The study session continues where it left off.

"So, Dawnece," Claire asks, "what did you do for *attendre?*"

"Well, since *attendre* means 'to wait,' I came up with, 'Each time I *attend* something, I have to *wait* in line before I get in.'"

"I came up with 'I can't *wait* to *attendre* in the driver's license line.' I think I like yours better."

Claire writes Dawnece's sentence in her notebook, and Karen decides to do likewise in her own notes. Even though Karen had gone through her flash cards less than an hour ago, she didn't remember what *attendre* means.

"Karen, what's your sentence for *attendre?*" Claire asks.

Karen doesn't have a sentence at all, but she tries to save face. "Um . . . mine's pretty much like Dawnece's."

"OK," Dawnece says, "the next word is *demander,* which means 'to request.'"

"Oh, I have a great one for that," Claire says. "'My mom's *requests* are more like *demands.*' *Demands* can remind me of *demander.*"

"Good one!" Dawnece exclaims. She and Karen both write the sentence in their notebooks.

"OK, the next word is *l'histoire,* which means 'story,'" Claire says. "How about, '*L'histoire,* or *history,* is a *story* about the world.'"

"That should be easy enough to remember," agrees Dawnece.

"Is this how you guys always study?" Karen asks. "Like, making up sentences for each new word?"

"Sure," Dawnece answers.

"First we put the word in an English sentence, and then we put it in a French phrase or sentence," Claire adds. "For *l'histoire,* we might say *a ce que dit l'histoire,* which means 'as the story goes . . . '"

"Wow!" says Karen. "What a good idea!"

Karen is nervous as Mr. Lanier passes out the French test, but she's determined to do well. "You can do this, you really can," she tells herself. She takes a deep breath and then looks at her test. "OK, the first word is *l'histoire*. Let's see, 'history is a story about the world,' so *l'histoire* means 'story.' OK, the second word is *demander.* Oh, yeah, 'my mom's requests are more like demands,' so *demander* means 'to request.' Hey, I *know* this stuff. I really know it!"

Karen quickly finishes the vocabulary portion of the test and then breezes through her translation of the assigned excerpt from *Candide*. She finishes the test in 35 minutes, several minutes before most of her classmates.

The following Monday, Mr. Lanier returns the graded test papers. On Karen's paper he's written "Good job!" across the top. On the back page of the test is an A– in bright red ink. She's answered all of her vocabulary words correctly, and she's made only a few minor mistakes in her translation of the *Candide* excerpt.

Questions for "Studying French"

1. *Claire and Dawnece appear to know far more about effective study strategies than Karen does—an advantage that can best be described as which one of the following?*
   a. *Social cognition*
   b. *Divergent thinking*
   c. *Formal operational reasoning*
   d. *More sophisticated metacognitive awareness*
2. *Using an information-processing perspective, characterize Karen's approach to studying French prior to her study session with her friends.*
3. *By using flash cards to study in French I, Karen apparently thinks that mastering French involves little more than memorizing vocabulary words. This perception is an example of which one of the following?*
   a. *Verbal mediation*
   b. *Convergent thinking*
   c. *An epistemological belief*
   d. *The sensory register in action*
4. *Karen worries that Dawnece might think she is stupid if she suggests that they study together. To some extent, Karen's concern may reflect what common phenomenon in early adolescence?*
   a. *The personal fable*
   b. *The imaginary audience*
   c. *A sense of self that has little basis in reality*
   d. *The inability of most adolescents to look at situations from their peers' perspectives*
5. *An **attribution** is an individual's causal explanation for a success or failure. To what does Karen attribute Claire's success in French?*

6. *Explain how Dawnece's and Claire's approach to studying French helps them encode and retrieve what they are studying.*
7. *Students' sense of self-efficacy affects their goals, their choice of activities, and their effort and persistence in classroom activities. Consequently, it also affects their learning and achievement. Describe how Karen's self-efficacy about learning French changes over the course of the case study and how it potentially affects her thinking and behavior.*
8. *As a teacher, what things might you do to help students develop effective study strategies?*

CASE 12
Pollution

When 14-year-old Laura arrives at school each morning, her first stop is the restroom, where she touches up her makeup and puts every loose hair back in place. She usually lingers for 10 or 15 minutes so that she can share the latest school gossip with her friends.

Laura's extended restroom visits often make her late for her first-hour study hall. When Ms. Watkins, the school counselor, chastises her for her consistent tardiness, Laura replies, "Everyone will notice if I don't look my absolute *best*. I don't want people to think I'm a geek!"

"Do you *like* people looking at you, Laura?" Ms. Watkins asks.

"Well, sure. I mean, everybody does, don't you think?"

Ms. Watkins smiles. "Yes, Laura, I think that almost everybody likes to have attention once in a while. Maybe that's just part of being human. And I know a class where you can be the center of attention—a class in which everyone wants to hear your opinion about things. Let's see if we can find a place for you in Mr. Marculescu's Debating I class. It meets first hour, the same time as your study hall. There's a catch, though. If you're late, then you won't have a chance to participate in any debates."

"No problem, Ms. Watkins. For something like that, I can certainly be on time if I need to."

The following morning, Mr. Marculescu begins class by saying, "Today we're going to practice one of the topics that we'll be debating next week with South High School's Debating I class. The topic is this: How do we solve the nation's pollution problems? We'll begin by having several of you get up in front of the class, one at a time, to present your ideas about how to deal with pollution. I'll pretend that I'm someone from the South High team and challenge each of you. Who would like to be our first volunteer?"

Not realizing what she might be getting herself into, Laura eagerly raises her hand.

"OK, Laura, you want to give it a shot? Come on up here and stand behind the podium on the right. I'll take the podium on the left."

"Can't I just stay here in my seat?"

"I'd prefer that you stand up here where everyone can see you and hear what you have to say."

As Laura approaches the front of the room, she begins to have second thoughts about joining this class. She decides to put up a good front by pretending that she knows what she's doing. She stands behind her assigned podium with the best air of confidence she can muster.

From behind his own podium, Mr. Marculescu addresses the other students: "Just a reminder about what the rest of you need to do here. As Laura presents her position regarding how we might solve the country's pollution problems, you should all be listening carefully for flaws in her arguments. OK, Laura, you may begin."

Laura hesitates as she looks around the room. "I . . . uh . . . I'm not sure I know what to say about this."

"Why don't you begin by talking about what you think the *causes* of pollution are?" Mr. Marculescu suggests. "I'm sure you have some good ideas, and we'd all like to hear them."

"You mean that you actually *care* what I say?" Laura asks.

"Of course," her new teacher assures her. "What you have to say is *definitely* important." Mr. Marculescu looks pointedly at her, waiting for her to begin.

She swallows hard and then says, "Well, I think the government shouldn't allow people to sell gasoline. That way, we wouldn't have any more air pollution from car exhaust or other machines."

"You mean, people shouldn't be able to sell gasoline to *anyone?*" Mr. Marculescu queries. "Not even to the mail carriers, the garbage collectors, the school bus drivers?"

"Right. People could take their garbage to the landfills as they walk to work. Some of them could run or ride bikes. Most people are too fat anyway, so the exercise would do them good."

"How much time do you think it would take a single mother with an infant and a child in elementary school to get to her job if she had to stop at a child care center, an elementary school, and a landfill on her way every day?"

"Oh, not too long. She could just put her kids in a covered bike carrier and throw the garbage bag on top of it. Besides, she wouldn't have to go to the landfill *every* day, only when the trash piles up."

"But while the trash is piling up at home, won't it attract mice and rats?"

"Well, then, I guess she would just have to go to the landfill more often."

"But what if her job is miles away from her house?"

"She should move, of course!"

"What about the elderly? How would they get their trash to the landfills?"

"They'd have their children or neighbors do it for them."

"But wouldn't the landfill itself cause some pollution?"

"Not really, because we could just have some scientist pour chemicals over it until it dissolves."

"Wouldn't the chemicals pollute our air and water?"

"Science is changing every day, and scientists are always learning new things. Maybe someone could find a new chemical that would get rid of all the bad things. It's possible, you know."

Mr. Marculescu continues to challenge Laura's reasoning, but the girl remains firmly convinced that her proposed ban on gasoline sales is a viable solution to the country's pollution problems, and she finds Mr. Marculescu's questions more annoying than enlightening. As she puts it so succinctly to her friends while restyling her hair in the restroom later that day, "Mr. Marculescu can be so *unreasonable!*"

Questions for "Pollution"

1. *Which one of Laura's behaviors is* **not** *necessarily typical of early adolescence?*
    a. *Her consistent tardiness*
    b. *Her belief that everyone is looking at her*
    c. *Her desire to spend time gossiping with friends*
    d. *Her overly simplistic and idealistic views of how to solve a real-world problem*
2. *From a developmental standpoint, how might we explain Laura's preoccupation with her appearance?*
3. *Below are four possible explanations for Laura's behavior. Which one is most consistent with a* **behaviorist** *(rather than cognitive) approach to learning and development?*
    a. *Laura's social goals seem to take precedence over her academic goals.*
    b. *Laura is focused on performance goals rather than on mastery goals.*
    c. *Because Laura hasn't been punished for her tardiness to study hall, this behavior continues unabated.*
    d. *Laura attributes Mr. Marculescu's series of challenging questions to a general "unreasonableness" on his part.*
4. *In suggesting that Laura join the debating class, Ms. Watkins is hoping to pique an interest in classroom subject matter by capitalizing on Laura's desire to be the center of attention. What other strategies might the school faculty use to motivate students who seem to be more interested in social matters than in academic pursuits?*
5. *From the perspective of Piaget's theory, in which stage of cognitive development is Laura?*
6. *How is Laura's reasoning affected by her knowledge base—that is, by what she does and doesn't know about pollution?*
7. *By posing a series of questions, Mr. Marculescu continually challenges Laura to reconsider her thinking about the pollution problem. What are potential benefits of this strategy?*
8. *In what ways might a debating class contribute to students' cognitive, linguistic, social, and moral development?*

CASE 13
The Reflection in the Window

Eight-year-old Jason seems to be staring out the window of his second-grade classroom. "Jason," Ms. Brown whispers, "you need to get back to the story you're writing with your spelling words." He nods, looks at the clock, then writes one more sentence on the paper in front of him. Within minutes, he is gazing out the window again. Ms. Brown sighs when she sees him off-task a second time. She walks over to him and asks, "Do you think you need to move closer to my desk, where there won't be any windows to distract you?"

"Maybe that would be a good idea," Jason whispers.

Jason's response surprises Ms. Brown. She had expected that her threat would entice him to finish his work. But instead she now has to follow through with the threat and find a place for him at the front of the room.

Midway through the morning, as his classmates enjoy recess outside, Jason remains in the classroom to work on assignments he could easily have completed before recess began. While he works at a table at the back of the room, Ms. Brown moves his desk so that it is just a few feet away from her own.

"Jason, this is the fourth time in a row you've missed out on morning recess, yet every day you spend even more time looking out the window than you did the day before. These consequences—missing recess and sitting next to me—are the only things I can think of to get you back on track."

"Oh, I don't mind, Ms. Brown. I'd rather be sitting near you than looking at your reflection in the window." He is grinning from ear to ear.

Ms. Brown is both stunned and flattered. After thinking for a moment, she approaches Jason, stoops down to his level and asks, "Why have you been watching me?"

"'Cause you're beautiful. I like to look at you."

"Oh, I see. Tell me, Jason, have you been staying in from recess on purpose?"

Jason looks down at his feet. "Yes," he whispers. "I love you, and it's the only time I get you all to myself." He then looks up at his teacher and asks, "Will you marry me, Ms. Brown . . . I mean, when I get big and everything?"

Ms. Brown smiles. "Jason, I would love to marry someone like you, but you see, I'm just not ready to get married."

"So when do you think you'll be ready?"

"Well, how about this? If you still want to marry me when you get big—bigger than me and old enough to grow a mustache—then we'll discuss it. OK?"

He smiles. "You know, I *will* marry you. I won't change my mind about that."

"Jason, you will always hold a special place in my heart. In the meantime, I like for my guys to fulfill their responsibilities. One of *your* responsibilities is to do your work when I assign it. OK?" Jason nods. "I wonder if we can think of another part of each day—not recess—when you and I could spend a little time together."

"Just me and you, you mean?" Jason asks.

Ms. Brown nods yes, then suggests, "How about if you become my morning helper? Your mom drives you to school every day, and most of the time, you're here at least 15 minutes before the first bell rings. Maybe you could help me get things ready in the classroom before school starts."

"Wow, that would be great! Can I start tomorrow, Ms. Brown?"

"Sure, if it's OK with your mom. Shall I call her this afternoon and see what she thinks?"

Jason's eyes light up, and he nods his head in enthusiastic agreement.

"But," Ms. Brown says, "there's just one little catch, Jason. I will let you be my morning helper *only* if you finish your work on time so that you can go to recess with the other children."

Jason offers his hand and replies, "It's a deal. Let's shake on it to make it official."

Questions for "The Reflection in the Window"

1. *Use a behaviorist perspective to explain why Jason isn't getting his work done.*
2. *Look at the case from the perspective of a behaviorist. When Ms. Brown moves Jason closer to her desk, she is _____ Jason's dawdling behavior.*
    a. *punishing*
    b. *positively reinforcing*
    c. *negatively reinforcing*
    d. *vicariously reinforcing*
3. *Ms. Brown makes at least two mistakes when she threatens to move Jason's desk near her own. What are they?*
4. *Jason appears to have a crush on Ms. Brown. How should Ms. Brown react to Jason's professed affection?*
5. *It isn't at all unusual for students to develop crushes on their teachers. What might you do if one of your students develops a crush on you?*
6. *Is it appropriate for Ms. Brown to give Jason extra attention each morning before school starts? Why or why not?*
7. *How might principles from sociocultural theory come into play as Jason helps Ms. Brown set up the classroom each morning?*

CASE 14
The Marble Jar

Of the 28 students in Mr. Fenwick's second-grade class, nine come from homes in which a language other than English is spoken. These students, plus four others who have been diagnosed as having learning disabilities, are reading at a preprimer (i.e., kindergarten) level or not at all, and many of them have not yet learned their basic addition and subtraction facts. Yet in the same class, Mr. Fenwick has another nine students who have been identified as being eligible for special services for the gifted and talented.

"I should be thankful," Mr. Fenwick tells himself. "Yes, it's a group with many academic deficiencies, but it's also a very *nice* group. There are no thieves, no pathological liars. Things could certainly be worse."

To accommodate the diverse academic needs of his class, Mr. Fenwick has his students working independently or in small groups much of the time so that they can all work on tasks tailored to their specific skill levels and needs. A number of students have difficulty staying on the tasks he's assigned, yet he is hardly in a position to keep his eye on everyone all of the time.

Although it's only October, Mr. Fenwick can already see behavior problems escalating in his classroom. He seeks the advice of the school psychologist, Ms. Rashad, and together they identify a strategy that Mr. Fenwick might be able to use with the entire class.

The following morning, Mr. Fenwick brings to school a large, empty jar and a bag of marbles. Holding the jar and marbles up for everyone to see, he says, "Boys and girls, I've brought this jar and these marbles to help us get our work done." When the children look puzzled, he adds, "Every time I see someone in the room doing what he or she is supposed to be doing, I will put a marble in the jar. I will also put one in every time I see someone doing something to help someone else learn."

Gillian raises her hand. "You mean, every time we learn something, we get a marble?"

"That's right," Mr. Fenwick responds. "And when the jar is full, the whole class gets a reward—perhaps an ice cream party, a field trip, or an afternoon of fun and games in the classroom."

"Cool!" several of the children shout. A couple of them exchange high-fives.

"What reward shall we work for the first time?" Mr. Fenwick asks. He writes a number of possibilities on the chalkboard. Through a series of votes, the children

---

This case is derived from an unpublished case study written by Barbara Day.

narrow down the choices and soon settle on a trip to the neighborhood firehouse as something that they would all enjoy.

In the days that follow, Mr. Fenwick keeps a lookout for appropriate and productive behaviors. Every time he drops a marble into the marble jar, he explains why he is doing so: "I see that all of you are hard at work on your reading assignments." "Thank you, Fernando, for helping James with his math problems." "You've all cleaned up your desks so nicely. Who would guess that just 5 minutes ago there were crayons, bottles of glue, and scraps of paper scattered everywhere!"

As the weeks roll on, Mr. Fenwick notices the children's classroom behaviors gradually improving. Eventually some behaviors occur so regularly that he decides he probably doesn't need to reinforce them as frequently as he has in the past. At the same time he adds new behaviors—for example, returning to one's seat promptly after recess, respecting other people's property, being a good listener—to his list of those that merit a marble when he sees them.

Questions for "The Marble Jar"

1. What basic principle of behaviorism is Mr. Fenwick using in this situation?
2. Characterize the nature of the reinforcement that Mr. Fenwick is using.
3. Why do you think the marble jar is effective in improving students' behavior in Mr. Fenwick's classroom?
4. Three of the following factors probably contribute to the effectiveness of the marble jar in improving the children's behaviors. Which one is **least** likely to be contributing to the improvement?
    a. Mr. Fenwick rewards a desired behavior immediately after it occurs.
    b. The children have a say in the particular reward for which they'll work.
    c. Mr. Fenwick tells the children specifically what they are doing to earn a marble.
    d. Mr. Fenwick stops rewarding a particular behavior after it begins to occur regularly.
5. After implementing the marble jar procedure, Mr. Fenwick sees some behaviors occurring regularly and decides that he doesn't need to reinforce them as frequently as he has in the past. Which concept from behaviorist theories of learning is Mr. Fenwick applying here?
    a. Generalization
    b. Primary reinforcement
    c. Classical conditioning
    d. Intermittent reinforcement
6. If Mr. Fenwick were to use a cognitive (rather than behaviorist) approach in motivating his students, what strategies might he use?
7. Mr. Fenwick has a diverse group of students, including some with limited knowledge of English, some with learning disabilities, and some who are gifted. Identify at least two different strategies a teacher might use to meet the needs of such a wide range of student ability levels.

CASE 15
Seven Chips

E. Jefferson Ingersoll III was born with neurofibromatosis, a neurological disorder sometimes (erroneously) called Elephant Man disease. Jefferson's disease has affected his appearance; his head is a bit larger than usual, and many internal lesions have left discolored patches of skin on his arms and legs. The disease has affected his behavior as well; he walks a little off-center, and his movement is almost invariably awkward and unbalanced.

Unfortunately, Jefferson's doctors have been unable to determine the severity of his condition. They have warned his mother that neurofibromatosis often becomes progressively debilitating as the years go by and that Jefferson may not live to adulthood. Ms. Ingersoll has responded by trying to give her son a lifetime's worth of gifts and attention in the few short years that she may have him. The result is that when Jefferson begins third grade in Ms. Stanton's classroom, he is an overindulged boy who seems completely unable to regulate his own behavior.

From the first day of school, it is clear that Jefferson wants nothing more than to be liked by his teacher and classmates. At the same time, he seems to do everything possible to undermine his chances of gaining anyone else's affection. For example, he often interrupts the flow of small-group and whole-class lessons with inappropriate comments, irrelevant questions, or unprovoked laughter. During any single independent activity, he sharpens his pencil at least five or six times, always taking the most indirect route possible to the pencil sharpener; as he does so, he often bumps into someone else, necessitating either an excessively loud apology or a denial that he is in any way responsible for the mishap. And throughout the day, Jefferson makes frequent trips to the drinking fountain and the restroom, always managing to disrupt classroom activities in the process.

At first Ms. Stanton tries to ignore Jefferson's inappropriate behaviors, thinking that such responses will gradually decrease if she refuses to acknowledge them. But when she sees no improvement in his behavior, she tries other, more assertive strategies. For example, she praises him when he is on-task and reprimands him for getting out of his seat, making inappropriate remarks, or in other ways disrupting classroom activities. On several occasions she meets with Jefferson and his mother to discuss the seriousness of the misbehaviors and to stress the importance of staying on-task and allowing other students to do likewise. At one point Ms. Stanton even develops a contingency contract for Jefferson, specifying desired behaviors in concrete terms and identifying the rewards that

This case is derived from an unpublished case study written by Barbara Day.

would follow such behaviors. Despite all her efforts, Jefferson's disruptive behaviors continue unabated.

While her class is at physical education one afternoon, Ms. Stanton seeks the advice of Mr. Manzini, the school psychologist. Together they decide that of all of Jefferson's misbehaviors, his continual movement around the classroom is the most disruptive and so must be dealt with first. Mr. Manzini suggests that Ms. Stanton give Jefferson seven plastic poker chips at the beginning of school each day. Whenever Jefferson gets out of his seat without permission, he must "pay" for this behavior with a chip. Once he's used all seven chips, he must remain in his seat for the rest of the morning; a single out-of-seat behavior at this point will result in his having to spend the next lunch and recess alone in a small room just off the main office.

The following morning Ms. Stanton tells Jefferson about the new procedure and gives him his first daily supply of chips. After that, whenever she sees him moving about the classroom without permission, she gets his attention and holds out her hand, and he obligingly gives her a chip. In the weeks that follow, Jefferson always limits his out-of-seat behaviors to the magic number seven. In fact, some days he doesn't even spend all of his chips. Ms. Stanton collects any extras at the end of each day and gives him a new pencil each time she's accumulated 25 of them.

Jefferson soon learns that if he gets out of his seat quietly and without disturbing his classmates, Ms. Stanton doesn't ask him for a chip. In fact, at one point, not only does she not request a chip, she also tells him, "I'm so pleased to see you moving quietly around the classroom, Jefferson."

Jefferson is immediately on the defensive. "It's OK for me to be out of my seat, Ms. Stanton. I still have a chip."

One day a few weeks later, Jefferson is working at the back of the classroom with Ms. Zhang, the speech pathologist. When Ms. Zhang asks him to speak more softly, he asks her what she means.

"Talk like you do when you're doing independent work," Ms. Zhang responds. "You know . . . *whisper!*"

Jefferson laughs. "I just do that so Ms. Stanton won't take a chip," he exclaims loudly. Only when Ms. Zhang assures him that she, too, can take a chip does he lower the volume of his voice.

As the school year draws to a close, Jefferson still doesn't seem to be able to regulate his own classroom behavior. The seven daily chips work wonders in helping him keep his behavior under control. But on occasions when he receives no chips first thing in the morning—for example, when Ms. Stanton is suddenly called out of town and doesn't have a chance to brief the substitute teacher—he reverts back to his loud and disruptive actions. And when Jefferson enters Mr. Quinlan's fourth-grade classroom the following year, he acts as if he has never seen a poker chip in his life.

Questions for "Seven Chips"

1. *Which one of the following parenting styles best characterizes the approach Jefferson's mother takes in raising her son?*
    a. *Permissive*
    b. *Uninvolved*
    c. *Authoritative*
    d. *Authoritarian*
2. *Using concepts and principles from behaviorism, provide a theoretical rationale for Ms. Stanton's chip strategy.*
3. *What evidence do you see that Ms. Stanton's strategy, although leading to a temporary improvement in Jefferson's behavior, is unlikely to have long-term effects?*
4. *A **contingency contract** is a formal written agreement between a teacher and a student that specifies acceptable behaviors the student will demonstrate and the reinforcers that a teacher will award for those behaviors. When Ms. Stanton develops a contingency contract for Jefferson, she violates one of the basic guidelines for such contracts. What mistake does she make?*
5. *Draw on research findings regarding the effective use of reinforcement and punishment in the classroom to describe how you might improve on Ms. Stanton's chip strategy.*
6. *Use concepts and principles related to **self-regulation** to develop an alternative approach Ms. Stanton might use to help Jefferson acquire more productive classroom behaviors.*
7. *Describe at least two different strategies Ms. Stanton might use to help Jefferson acquire better social skills.*
8. *If you had a student with neurofibromatosis in your classroom, what would you do to prepare for this student and help him or her to be academically and socially successful?*

CASE 16
Throwing Tantrums

Although Tyler Lipton is listed on the roster of Allie Schenk's third-grade class, he spends most of each day in Sharon Osmer's resource room. Concerned that Tyler is so often segregated from his classmates, Allie has arranged a meeting with Sharon Osmer, Principal Cecelia Dawson, and Tyler's parents.

Allie begins the meeting: "I'm uncomfortable with the fact that Tyler is away from my classroom as much as he is. He's missing many of our instructional activities, and he has few opportunities to make friends with the other children in the class."

"Our son is severely dyslexic," explains Mr. Lipton, Tyler's father. "He's already repeated first grade, and now he's repeating the second-grade reading curriculum as well, yet he still can't read. I'd like him to spend as much time with Ms. Osmer as he possibly can."

"I worry about his behavior, too," Ms. Lipton adds. "Sometimes Tyler gets so frustrated that he throws horrible temper tantrums. It would never work to have him in a classroom with 25 other students. He needs as much individual attention as he can get."

Sharon Osmer is quick to agree. "Yes, Tyler's in my room so that we can address both his dyslexia and his behavior problems. I've had him for 2 years now, but his behavior is becoming even worse than it used to be. For example, he breaks pencils and tears his paper to shreds when he's frustrated or angry. Sometimes he screams when he doesn't want to do his work."

"Didn't Tyler's screaming start at about the same time that you started working with Marcus?" Allie asks.

Sharon thinks for a minute. "Well, yes, now that you mention it, that's true."

"Who's Marcus?" inquires Ms. Lipton.

"Marcus is a boy with autism who's in my room all day long," Sharon replies. "He frequently screams and flaps his arms, especially when he's frustrated. Such behavior is pretty typical for a child with autism."

"What do you do when Marcus screams?" Allie asks Sharon.

"Well, as you know, I almost always have several students in my room at the same time, and each one of them is likely to have different academic needs. I usually give them individual assignments and put them at separate workstations around the room, then I circulate and give everyone a few minutes of one-on-one instruction. When Marcus gets too noisy, I pass out earplugs so the other students can concentrate on what they're doing. Then I try to find out why Marcus is so upset. He usually settles down after I've spent a little time with him."

"This meeting's about Tyler," Principal Dawson reminds the group. "I think we should keep Marcus out of the discussion."

"Well, let me explain why I brought Marcus up," Allie says. "I talked with Kendra Westover, who had Tyler in her classroom 2 years ago, and she doesn't remember him ever screaming in her classroom. She told me that he was placed in the resource room only for his reading problems, *not* for any behavior problems. So I'm wondering . . . could it be that Tyler has learned to scream in your classroom, Sharon? After being with Marcus so much, he may think it's OK to scream when he's frustrated."

"Hmmm . . . that's an interesting idea," Ms. Lipton says. "Now that I think about it, I realize that Tyler's temper tantrums didn't really start until this year. Before that, he usually just talked to us when he was upset about something."

"I've been attributing his screaming more to his decreasing self-confidence," Mr. Lipton says. "Tyler's 9 years old, and yet he still has trouble reading even the simplest words. He certainly doesn't feel good about that."

"I've been worried about his self-esteem as well," Sharon replies. "I've tried to boost it a bit by assigning him tasks that are easy for him. You know, completing color-by-number worksheets, listening to stories—things he can do successfully by himself. Yet his screaming seems to have increased rather than decreased."

"Sharon, you do wonderful things with the children you have in your resource room," Allie tells her. "But it sounds to me as if Marcus's behavior is rubbing off on Tyler. I'd like to suggest that we move Tyler back into my classroom for most of the school day. Perhaps you could give me some ideas about how I could help him with his reading skills."

"But you're forgetting about Tyler's behavior, Allie," Cecelia Dawson points out. "Tyler's a very disruptive kid, and his presence in your room would be a great distraction. You must remember your other students. After all, they have a right to a classroom environment in which they can reasonably get some work done."

"It seems to me that Tyler needs to see how *normal* children behave," Allie observes. "I have a really good group this year—not a serious behavior problem in the bunch. How is Tyler ever going to learn appropriate classroom behavior when he's in a room with kids like Marcus all day?"

"I think you're being unrealistic, Allie," Cecelia says. "Tyler may feel ostracized when you put him with children who can read and write. By putting him in your classroom all day, we might destroy what little self-esteem he has."

"But there are many things Tyler would be perfectly capable of doing in my classroom. For example, he could participate in science experiments. The children conduct the experiments in pairs, and he could certainly contribute. During reading times, he could listen to the other students read aloud and get involved in group discussions. And I see no reason why he shouldn't participate in physical education, art, and music along with his classmates."

Seeing that Allie is getting a bit hot under the collar, Cecelia tries to calm her down. "Now, Allie, I wasn't intending to ruffle any feathers. I'm just trying to point out that the approach you're suggesting might not be as easy as you think it will be."

Allie turns to Mr. and Ms. Lipton. "I have no idea what I can or cannot do for your son," she tells them bluntly. "I'm certainly no miracle worker. But it's clear that Tyler needs to learn to deal with his frustrations appropriately, and he can do that only if he interacts with regular kids on a regular basis. All I'm asking for is a chance to work with him. Will you at least think about it?"

❖❖❖

Mr. and Ms. Lipton *do* think about it, and in a formal staffing later that month, the decision is made to place Tyler in Allie Schenk's room for most of the school day. For a half-hour each morning, when his classmates are meeting in their reading groups, Tyler will go to the resource room to work with Sharon Osmer on his reading skills.

In the 3 weeks since Tyler joined Allie Schenk's class, he has neither screamed nor torn up his work. He still can't read or write at the same level that his classmates do—a continuing source of frustration for him. But he's making many new friends and cooperating well with others during group activities.

When Allie asks Tyler why he used to scream in Ms. Osmer's class, his response is quite revealing: "Well, wouldn't you get pretty upset if you had to do the same stupid worksheets and listen to the same dumb stories all day—*every* day—while everyone else in your class gets to do new and exciting stuff?"

Note: Tyler had special assistance with reading throughout his schooling. He graduated with his age-mates in the spring of 1997.

Questions for "Throwing Tantrums"

1. *Tyler has dyslexia. Which one of the following characteristics is most often associated with this condition?*
   a. *Difficulty in hearing the individual sounds in words*
   b. *Low self-efficacy about all academic content domains*
   c. *Writing letters or words as mirror images of themselves*
   d. *Little understanding of commonly used words in spoken language*
2. *In the United States, the Individuals with Disabilities Education Act (IDEA) gives children with disabilities a right to all of the following **except** which one?*
   a. *Fair and nondiscriminatory evaluation*
   b. *An individualized educational program*
   c. *Education in the least restrictive environment*
   d. *Special tutoring and extra time for all assignments*
3. *Sharon Osmer tries to enhance Tyler's self-esteem by giving him tasks that she knows he can accomplish successfully (e.g., color-by-number worksheets), yet Tyler's self-esteem continues to decrease. Why?*
4. *Taking into account Vygotsky's concept of the **zone of proximal development**, explain why the tasks that Sharon Osmer assigns to Tyler are developmentally inappropriate.*
5. *Using concepts from social cognitive theory, explain how Tyler has acquired the screaming behavior.*

6. *What advantages are there in placing Tyler in Allie Schenk's classroom for most or all of the school day?*
7. *If you were Tyler's teacher, what strategies might you use to accommodate his special needs?*
8. *Concerned that Tyler's academic needs are not being met, Allie schedules a meeting with the special education teacher, the school principal, and Tyler's parents. Is this an appropriate strategy? Why or why not?*

CASE 17
The Distracting Influence

Ms. Johnson has just convened the Gorillas, one of the reading groups in her fourth-grade class. "OK, children," she begins, "yesterday we started a new book, *The Phantom Tollbooth,* by Norton Juster. Who can summarize what happened to Milo in Chapter 1?"

As one of the Gorillas provides a summary for the group, Ms. Johnson overhears Nicole and Ashley talking and giggling at the front of the room. The girls should instead be silently reading Louis Sachar's *Wayside School Is Falling Down.* In fact, Ashley, who is visually impaired, has a Braille version of the book lying open in front of her.

Ms. Johnson doesn't mind if her students occasionally talk with one another when a reading group is meeting, as long as they do so quietly and are able to finish their assigned reading before recess. But Nicole has a habit of talking so much that she doesn't get her work done, and Ms. Johnson must often keep her in at recess to finish it.

Attempting to discourage Nicole's excessive chattiness, Ms. Johnson has moved the child's desk three times in the past 2 months. After the first move, Nicole sat next to Raul, a shy, quiet boy who always did his work. Unfortunately, Raul began modeling Nicole's behavior (rather than vice versa), and within a couple of weeks the two children were talking and laughing most of their mornings away, to the point where Ms. Johnson was keeping them *both* in at recess to finish their schoolwork.

Ms. Johnson then moved Nicole to the other side of the room, seating her next to Peter. Although now a more sociable child than before, Raul was once again completing his assignments. In the meantime, Peter, rejected by most of his classmates as being too much of a bully, delighted in the friendship that Nicole offered him. In one respect, Nicole was a positive influence on him, showing him how to engage in friendly small talk with his peers. But like Raul, Peter usually became so engrossed in his daily conversations with Nicole that his classwork began to suffer.

Trying to harness Nicole's gift of gab, Ms. Johnson has finally moved her to the front of the room to sit by Ashley, hoping that Nicole could become a "tutor" of sorts, describing things that Ashley could not see. Today, for example, Nicole might describe the pictures in *Wayside School Is Falling Down.* But the girls' conversation today seems to be about rollerblading, rather than about the book. It's becoming increasingly clear that Nicole cannot keep her mind on her schoolwork no matter whom she sits with, and that, furthermore, she will always be pulling someone else off-task as well.

After wrapping up the Gorillas' discussion of new vocabulary words in *The Phantom Tollbooth,* Ms. Johnson distributes index cards to each of her students. "Before I convene the Tigers' group," she tells the class, "I'd like for us to talk about a problem we seem to be having during reading group time. Some of you are off-task too much when you're supposed to be working independently. What do I mean when I say *off-task?*"

"Like talking to a friend," Aaron replies.

"Or sharpening our pencils all the time," Deion adds.

"Getting too many drinks at the fountain," Amanda says.

"Those are all good answers," Ms. Johnson observes. "*Off-task* behaviors are the things you do that keep you from getting your work done. On the card I just gave each of you, I want you to make a checkmark every time you find yourself being off-task while I'm working with the Tigers. Then do the same thing again while I'm working with the Pandas. This isn't a contest to see who has the most or the fewest checkmarks. It's just my way of helping you to help *yourselves* get your work done. It will also help you see exactly what you do with your time. Do you have any questions?"

"Will we get in trouble if our checkmarks show we're off-task a lot?" Nicole asks.

"No, Nicole," Ms. Johnson replies. "Your cards are your own business; you don't even have to show them to me. It will be up to you if you want to share them with anyone or not."

Just before morning recess, Ms. Johnson says, "OK, now count up the number of checkmarks on your card. Let's go around the room and see how many checkmarks each one of you has. If you don't feel like sharing your number with the class, that's fine too."

"Zero," says Janice.

"Two . . . well, three if you count going to the bathroom," says Bobby. The class laughs.

"Three."

"Two."

"Three."

"Zero."

"Zero."

"One."

Except for Nicole, all of the children announce how often they have been off-task. The maximum number of checkmarks for any of them is three.

"You've been keeping track of your behavior for about an hour," Ms. Johnson says. "Do you think you were off-task very much during that time?"

"No," most of the children shout. Ms. Johnson sees that Nicole is quiet and looking down at her desk.

Ignoring Nicole, Ms. Johnson smiles. "I think you're right. Most of you were using your time wisely this morning. It's pretty neat to find out that you're doing your work without someone having to remind you all the time, isn't it?" After the children nod their heads in agreement, she continues, "Sometimes it's OK to be off-task, like when you have to go to the bathroom. But sometimes it's *not* OK, like when you distract one of your classmates by talking too much. Next time you find yourself off-task, ask yourself, 'Is it worth it to do what I'm doing right now? Is it worth it to lose my recess time or to have to take my schoolwork home to do just because I want to goof off now?'"

While her classmates are playing outside, Nicole has, as usual, remained inside to finish up her reading. Ms. Johnson walks over to Nicole's desk and sits down beside her. "I wonder how you did with your checkmarks. Would you like to share your score with me?"

"Not really."

"You know, Nicole, the first step in changing a bad habit is awareness. If you aren't aware of what you're doing, you can't change your behavior. But my guess is that when you started keeping track of how often you were off-task, you discovered that you were goofing off most of the time. Is goofing off really worth missing part of recess every day?"

"Ms. Johnson, until today . . . until we did the checkmark thing . . . I never realized *why* I was staying in from recess every day. I've always thought it took me longer to do my work because I'm not smart."

Ms. Johnson looks surprised. "Has anyone ever *told* you that you weren't smart?"

"No. It's just that . . . well, ever since first grade, it seems as if I've always missed recess, or at least part of it, every day."

"Boy, that's an awful lot of recesses to be missing, isn't it? You know, I bet that once you start buckling down, you'll find that you're a pretty smart girl after all. What do *you* think?" Ms. Johnson pauses and looks Nicole straight in the eye. "Do you think you can try to keep yourself on-task more often?"

"Yes!" Nicole replies. "I'm never going to talk in class again!"

"Well, that might be asking a lot of yourself, never to talk at *all*. But I would like you to continue keeping track of your own behavior during reading group time. How about if I let you borrow a digital timer I have that makes a little beep every 5 minutes? Each time you hear the beep, think about what you were just doing. If you weren't doing what you were *supposed* to be doing, then give yourself a checkmark."

"OK. That seems easy enough."

"Well, I don't know if it will be *easy,* but I certainly know that you can do it."

In the days that follow, Nicole finds that she makes fewer and fewer checkmarks on her card. And after 2 weeks of monitoring her own behavior, Nicole enjoys her first full period of recess. By the third week, she no longer keeps tally cards. She is now able to stay on-task regularly, and she hardly ever disturbs her classmates.

Questions for "The Distracting Influence"

1. *Ms. Johnson asks if someone in the Gorilla group can summarize what happened to Milo in Chapter 1 of* The Phantom Tollbooth. *This request reflects which level in Bloom's taxonomy?*

2. *Prior to using the tally cards, what strategies does Ms. Johnson use to try to curb Nicole's off-task behavior?*

3. *Is it appropriate to keep Nicole in from recess as a punishment for not completing her classwork?*

4. *When Ms. Johnson moves Nicole next to Raul—who's initially a very shy, quiet student—Raul soon begins talking and laughing instead of doing his schoolwork. Ms. Johnson soon holds both students in at recess to finish their classwork, but Raul continues to talk and laugh in class instead of completing his work. Which one of the following phenomena best explains this change in Raul's behavior?*
   a. *Modeling*
   b. *Elaboration*
   c. *Vicarious punishment*
   d. *Reciprocal causation*

5. *Explain the effectiveness of the checkmark strategy with regard to components of self-regulation it may foster.*

6. *Is it appropriate for Ms. Johnson to ask her students to read their scores in the checkmark exercise aloud to the class?*

7. *Characterize Nicole's self-efficacy with regard to academic tasks.*

8. *Nicole erroneously believes that she has been staying in during recess because of a lack of intelligence. Explain this belief using what you know about children's **attributions**.*

9. *If you had a student like Nicole, what other strategies might you use?*

CASE 18
A Silent World

Fed up with the fast-paced lifestyle of southern California, Lynn Budzynski and her 10-year-old daughter Becky have just moved to Sugar Springs, a small town in the Rocky Mountains. Two days after their arrival, Ms. Budzynski brings her daughter to Sugar Springs Elementary School. She fills out the paperwork to enroll Becky, then asks Ms. Bohlender, the school secretary, if she can speak with the interpreter for students with hearing impairments.

After pausing to think for a moment, Ms. Bohlender smiles and says, "Why don't you both have a seat? Let me see if I can find someone to meet with you."

Ms. Budzynski turns to her daughter and repeats, both orally and in American Sign Language, what the secretary has just said, then mother and daughter sit down on a couch by the office doorway. Ms. Bohlender disappears down a hallway behind the counter and returns soon after with a man whom she introduces as Mr. Hardwick, the school principal.

Mr. Hardwick smiles at Ms. Budzynski and Becky. "Welcome to Sugar Springs Elementary School. I'm afraid that we don't have an interpreter at our school right now, but I'll get on the phone this morning to make arrangements for one. In the meantime, let's get Becky started in her classroom so she can get acquainted with her new teacher and classmates. I think the best place to put her might be in Mr. Matherson's fifth-grade class."

Mr. Matherson is caught completely off guard when Becky arrives at his door a short time later. As someone who has grown up in the same small town in which he now teaches, he has never before met someone who is deaf; as a result, he has no idea how to communicate with his new student. While Becky stands at the front of the room waiting for instructions on where to sit, she watches her new teacher push a button in a metal box on the wall and then speak to it.

While Mr. Matherson is busy with the box, Becky observes the other children in the room. Some of them are talking with one another, whereas others are staring at her. She jumps, startled, when her teacher comes up behind her and unexpectedly puts his hand on her shoulder. The other children seem amused by her reaction. Mr. Matherson looks at her and points toward the door.

"Oh, whew!" Becky thinks. "I'm in the wrong place." She starts to walk out the door, but her departure is blocked by a desk that the custodian is carrying in. As she tries to walk around him, Mr. Matherson grabs her by the arm. The custodian sets the desk in the front row, winks at her, and walks out of the room. Mr. Matherson gestures for Becky to sit down at her new desk.

Before Becky arrived, the class had been in the middle of a lesson on long division, and the lesson now resumes. Seeing that the other children have their math books open on their desks, Becky signs for a textbook of her own. Mr. Matherson shrugs his shoulders to indicate that he doesn't know what she wants. Becky points to another child's book and then to herself. Mr. Matherson smiles and hands her a math book from a pile on the bookshelf.

Mr. Matherson says something to the class, then he writes a long division problem on the chalkboard. He slowly works through the problem, talking to the class as he does so. The other students occasionally nod their heads to indicate that they understand what he is showing them; observing their actions, Becky nods as well. Because she mastered the process of long division last year in California, she has no trouble understanding the process her teacher is demonstrating.

Mr. Matherson writes three more long division problems on the board. Becky sees several of the other children raising their hands, so she raises her hand as well. Mr. Matherson calls on two other children, who go to the board and begin working on the first two problems. Mr. Matherson then points to Becky, motions for her to come forward, and directs her to the third problem. Understanding what she is supposed to do, Becky grabs a piece of chalk and solves the problem with ease. As she and the other two children return to their seats, the girl sitting behind Becky smiles at her and gives her a "thumbs up" sign.

Mr. Matherson talks to the class for a few minutes longer and then stops. Becky sees her classmates pull sheets of paper out of their desks and begin to write down several long division problems. She gives Mr. Matherson a puzzled look because she doesn't know where the problems are coming from. Finally realizing that his new student would not have heard the instructions he just presented, he writes on the chalkboard: "Do problems 8–20 on pages 58 and 59."

Becky pulls a sheet of notebook paper from her backpack and quickly completes the assigned problems. When she is finished, she looks around the room and sees that most of her classmates are still hard at work. After waiting patiently for a few minutes, she leans across the aisle to see how the boy next to her is doing. Mr. Matherson comes up to her, puts his hand on her shoulder, waves his index finger back and forth, shakes his head no, and then points to her paper.

Not understanding, Becky gazes at a bulletin board at the side of the room until Mr. Matherson walks away. Then she gently tugs at the shirt of the boy beside her in an attempt to get his attention. He doesn't seem to notice her, so she tugs his shirt a little harder. When he still doesn't look her way, she smacks him on the arm in desperation and points to an incorrect math problem. The boy yelps in pain and pushes Becky away from him. Mr. Matherson is instantly at Becky's side once again. She smiles at him as she watches him move his lips and shake his finger at her. Although she's confused by her teacher's reaction, she's pleased that she's finally learned how to get people's attention.

Suddenly, the children head for the back door. Before Becky can get out of her seat to join them, she feels a familiar hand on her shoulder. Mr. Matherson motions for her to remain at her desk while the other children leave the room. Through the open door, she can see playground equipment and so correctly guesses that it's time for recess. Yet Mr. Matherson insists that she sit at her desk for several minutes before he lets her go outside. She doesn't understand why she has to miss some of her recess.

When Becky finally joins her classmates outside, she surveys the school grounds. She sees most of the girls in her class standing in small groups and talking. Because she has no way of communicating with them, she decides not to approach them. Instead, she walks over to the swings and stands beside a girl in a red jacket to wait for a turn. She gently touches the girl's sleeve, but the girl doesn't seem to notice her. Becky pinches the girl to get her attention; the girl turns around with a scowl and then says something while holding her fist close to Becky's face. Becky is delighted to get the girl's attention and so smiles at her new "friend." When the girl turns to talk to someone else, Becky pinches her again. This time the girl runs to Mr. Matherson and points to Becky.

Over the next 3 days, Mr. Matherson continues to see instances of inappropriate behavior in Becky's actions. For example, she frequently looks at her classmates' work, a response that he interprets as cheating. In addition, her hitting and pinching other children to get their attention seems to have escalated. Mr. Matherson has used a variety of strategies in an effort to discourage the problem behaviors—he has tried tapping her on the shoulder, shaking his head, scolding her, keeping her in the classroom during recess—but nothing seems to be making a difference. He's at a loss as to what to do next.

During lunch time of Becky's fourth day at her new school, a young woman appears at the cafeteria door and speaks briefly to Mr. Matherson. She then approaches Becky, stoops down, and signs, "Hi, I'm Miss Hunter. I'm your new interpreter. Instead of going to the playground after lunch today, how about if you stay inside with me so that we can get to know each other?"

Smiling, Becky signs, "OK."

Becky is delighted that she finally has someone with whom she can communicate. She has many questions to ask, but she starts with the one that's puzzling her the most: "Why do I have to stay in from recess every day? Is it because my teacher doesn't like me?"

"I'm sure that Mr. Matherson likes you very much, Becky," Miss Hunter responds. "I don't know why he's keeping you in from recess. Perhaps we should ask him."

When the other students return from their lunch break, Becky goes back to her seat. As the afternoon's lessons proceed, Miss Hunter continually uses her hands to interpret what Mr. Matherson and the other students are saying.

At one point during a lesson on air pollution, Mr. Matherson asks, "What happens when fog and smoke in the air mix together?" Miss Hunter translates the question for Becky, and Becky quickly shoots her hand in the air. Mr. Matherson points in her direction. She signs to Miss Hunter, who translates for the class, "We get smog."

Mr. Matherson smiles at her and says something in response, which Miss Hunter signs as, "Good job, Becky. You're the only one who knew that."

Becky beams with pleasure and signs back to Miss Hunter, "Anybody from California would know that!"

After school, Mr. Matherson and Miss Hunter finally have a few minutes to touch base on how the two of them can help Becky change her inappropriate social behaviors. "She's trying to make new friends, but she hasn't had any luck," Miss Hunter explains. "For example, she told me that the other day she tried to help the boy next to her with his long division, but it only seemed to upset both him and you. I think that perhaps Becky just wants to interact with her classmates and doesn't know how to go about doing it."

"So maybe *that's* why she's been hitting and pinching the other kids so much," Mr. Matherson responds. "We . . . the children and I . . . thought that Becky was being too aggressive. We need to do something to help Becky and her classmates communicate more effectively."

"How about if I teach you and the other kids to sign?" Miss Hunter suggests.

The following morning, Miss Hunter begins the first of what will be many 30-minute lessons in American Sign Language and finger spelling. Among the first sentences that Miss Hunter teaches the class are, "Would you like to play with me?" and "Would you help me?" She also teaches them to coach Becky on more appropriate attention-getting behavior by saying such things as, "That's not nice. *This* is what friends do . . . "

At recess a short time later, Becky pinches a boy on the monkey bars. He immediately turns to her to sign, "That's not nice." He takes Becky's hand, places it on the monkey bars, then signs, "Better. Friends play together—not hurt each other."

Questions for "A Silent World"

1. *What instances of modeling are evident in the case study?*
2. *On what occasion does Becky's behavior illustrate that she is accustomed to somewhat different standards for classroom behavior than exist in Mr. Matherson's class?*
3. *Before Miss Hunter joins her in the classroom, Becky has difficulty getting the attention of her teacher and classmates. She soon learns that hitting and pinching her classmates gains that attention. Mr. Matherson tries to discourage this*

behavior by keeping her in from recess, shaking his head, and scolding her, but her aggressive behaviors increase rather than decrease. Looking at the situation as an instance of operant conditioning, you can reasonably conclude that Mr. Matherson's reactions to Becky's aggressive behavior are serving as which one of the following?

    a. Punishment

    b. Positive reinforcement

    c. Negative reinforcement

    d. Vicarious reinforcement

4. *Why are Mr. Matherson's attempts to punish Becky not being effective?*

5. *In the first few days after Becky's arrival, how might Mr. Matherson and other school staff better help Becky make the transition to her new school and classroom?*

6. *In the United States, which component of Public Law 94-142 (IDEA) grants Becky the right to have an interpreter with her in the classroom?*

    a. Due process

    b. A free and appropriate education

    c. The least restrictive environment

    d. Fair and nondiscriminatory evaluation

7. *What are the potential benefits of teaching the other students American Sign Language and finger spelling?*

CASE 19
Topography

Less than a week before the school year begins, Ms. Steinbach receives a telephone call from Ms. Rocco, the principal at Oceanside Middle School. "I'd like to offer you a job teaching social studies," Ms. Rocco tells her. "Are you interested?"

"Why, yes, I am," Ms. Steinbach answers, trying to keep her excitement from being too obvious in her voice.

"That's wonderful news," Ms. Rocco responds. "I was very impressed when I interviewed you last spring, but at the time I didn't think we'd be needing another social studies teacher. As it turns out, Mr. Richardson, whom I believe you met during your interview, has resigned at the last minute to take an assistant principal position in another district."

The two women meet the same afternoon so that Ms. Steinbach can sign her contract and learn about the responsibilities of her new position. Ms. Rocco tells Ms. Steinbach that, among other things, she will be teaching two sessions of geography every morning. "Mr. Richardson ordered new geography textbooks for this year. I believe there are two boxes of them stacked beside the door in your classroom."

Ms. Steinbach thanks her new principal and hurries to her classroom, well aware that she has many hours of planning and preparation ahead of her over the next few days. The two boxes of geography texts are exactly where Ms. Rocco had said they would be. Opening one of the boxes, she finds a teacher's manual resting on top of about 20 textbooks.

Sitting at her new desk, Ms. Steinbach grabs a copy of the textbook. As she flips through the pages, she is dismayed at what she sees. Each chapter seems to be mostly a collection of facts listed one after another in rapid succession. New concepts—*plateau, tundra,* the *Continental Divide*—are briefly defined but rarely explained in any detail. Little attempt is made to pull all the facts and concepts together into a coherent whole.

When Ms. Steinbach opens the teacher's manual, she is even more discouraged. The classroom activities it describes focus on basic skills—identifying cardinal directions (north, southeast, etc.), interpreting simple bar graphs, using scales to estimate distance—that she suspects her students may have already mastered. The homework assignments that the manual provides are fill-in-the-blank exercises based on word-for-word excerpts from the textbook. And the quizzes for each chapter include only true-false and multiple-choice items.

Having taken several geography courses in her undergraduate program, Ms. Steinbach knows perfectly well that geography involves much more than facts and figures. She wants her students to learn broad geographic principles that they can use to make better sense of the world around them. The textbook and teacher's manual aren't going to help her meet this objective, so she decides to get busy developing alternative lessons and activities.

❖❖❖

Throughout the fall, Ms. Steinbach tries a number of different strategies to make geographic principles come alive for her students. For example, when teaching students about topography, she brings in several raised relief maps and gives the class a "scavenger hunt" list of landforms (mountain ranges, plateaus, river valleys, foothills) to locate on the maps. When teaching her class about volcanic activity, she borrows a series of slides from the local university's geography department to depict what Mount St. Helens looked like before and after its eruption in 1980. During hurricane season, Ms. Steinbach uses the Internet to locate the National Weather Service's daily updates regarding the location and status of current tropical storms and hurricanes and then has her students plot the course of each weather system on a large map of the Atlantic Ocean and eastern seaboard states.

On another occasion, after puzzling for several days about how she can make the effects of elevation on rainfall more concrete than the textbook's explanation, Ms. Steinbach conducts a rather unusual activity. "OK, class," she begins, "I need five volunteers to help us learn why the western side of a mountain usually gets more rainfall than the eastern side."

Many hands go up. Ms. Steinbach selects several of the more reserved students in her class—Angela, Miguel, Raymond, Tara, and Dee.

As the five volunteers walk to the front of the room, Ms. Steinbach places a bowl of water on the floor. "This bowl is the Pacific Ocean. Angela, your name is perfect for what you need to do, because I want you to be Los Angeles. Lie down just to the right of the bowl, please, because Los Angeles is a city that lies just to the east of the Pacific Ocean." The class snickers a bit as Angela obligingly lies on the floor beside the bowl.

"Miguel," Ms. Steinbach continues, "I'd like you to be the San Gabriel Mountains that rise up just to the northeast of Los Angeles." She gently moves Miguel so that he is standing to the right of Angela. "There, that's good. Just be careful that you don't step on Los Angeles." Again the class snickers.

Ms. Steinbach now looks at her third volunteer. "Raymond, I'd like you to be Barstow, a town that lies in the flatlands to the east of the San Gabriel Mountains." Immediately comprehending the nature of her request, Raymond lies down to the right of where Miguel is standing.

"Perfect!" Ms. Steinbach exclaims. "OK, class, here we have southern California. You see before you the Pacific Ocean—the bowl of water—then Los Angeles, the San Gabriel Mountains, and the town of Barstow on the other side." She looks quickly at her students and notes that their eyes are all focused on the front of the room in eager anticipation of what will happen next.

"So now we need a cloud and some wind. Tara, let's make you the wind. Stand over to the left of the bowl there, somewhere out in the middle of the ocean. And Dee, I'd like you to be a cloud." Ms. Steinbach hands Dee a sponge and nudges her to a spot directly in front of the bowl. "As a cloud, you hold quite a bit of the water vapor that's evaporated from the Pacific Ocean. So take your sponge and suck up some of the water from the ocean." Dee stoops down, puts the sponge in the bowl, and then stands up with a saturated, dripping "cloud."

"Excellent. So then, here we have an air mass full of water—a cloud—just hanging out over the Pacific Ocean. And then along comes the prevailing wind, the wind from the west, to move the cloud eastward. OK, wind, blow away!"

Tara dutifully blows on Dee's shoulder, and Dee walks slowly to the "east," holding the sponge over "Los Angeles" as she does so. Angela grimaces but says nothing as a few drops of water land on her face. Just before Dee reaches the "San Gabriel Mountains" that are Miguel, Ms. Steinbach stops her.

"Now here's where things get interesting, folks. Notice that the cloud has to rise as it travels over the mountains. As it does so, it's going to get *cooler* and *smaller,* and it won't be able to hold as much water. So what happens?"

"It'll start to rain!" Luke shouts out.

"Good, Luke. So Tara, let's get the wind going again. And Dee, let's make that cloud smaller and smaller as it starts to go over the San Gabriel Mountains." Tara resumes her blowing, and Dee slowly moves to the right once again, squeezing the sponge harder and harder as she does so. Angela and Miguel are being "rained" on in the process, but they are clearly enjoying the attention they are getting from their peers.

"Now the cloud starts going back down on the east side of the San Gabriel Mountains and gets warmer again. What happens to the rain?"

"It stops!" Kathleen calls out.

"Right!" Picking up on her cue, Dee stops squeezing the sponge as Tara "blows her" to where Raymond is lying. "So look at poor Barstow. It's dry as a bone. Has anyone here ever been to Barstow, California?"

"I have," Kenneth responds. "My dad and I go there sometimes for the all-terrain vehicle races."

"What's it like in Barstow, Kenneth?"

"Well, there's lots of sand and gravel, and hardly any trees. Like you just said, Ms. Steinbach, it's dry as a bone."

"Exactly." Ms. Steinbach looks pointedly at Raymond, who is still lying on the floor to the right of Miguel. "Mr. 'Barstow' here is in the Mojave Desert."

Questions for "Topography"

1. *Why is Ms. Steinbach so discouraged when she looks at the textbook and teacher's manual that Mr. Richardson ordered?*
2. *What strategies does Ms. Steinbach use to help her students learn effectively?*
3. *What strategies does Ms. Steinbach use to motivate her students and keep their attention?*
4. *Ms. Steinbach intentionally chooses some of the more reserved students to participate in the rainfall demonstration. What might be her rationale for doing so?*
5. *Which one of the following incidents in the case most clearly illustrates the process of **elaboration**?*
   a. *Dee soaks up water in the sponge.*
   b. *Kenneth recalls what Barstow's terrain is like.*
   c. *Kathleen correctly predicts that the rain will stop.*
   d. *Miguel positions himself to represent the San Gabriel Mountains.*
6. *Ms. Steinbach uses some rather creative strategies for making geography "come alive" for her students. What resources might you use to identify and develop equally creative strategies for teaching your own students?*

CASE 20
Consequences

"OK, class, it's time to turn in your spelling crossword puzzles," Ms. Wyatt announces to her sixth-grade class.

"But I didn't finish mine," Nicholas complains.

"Neither did I," says Derek.

"Of course not!" Eldrick shouts out. "You guys were too busy talking about Cindy Crawford!"

"Well, you have to admit, she *is* something to talk about," Nicholas responds with a smirk.

Ms. Wyatt shakes her head in mock disgust. "Apparently puberty is settling in here, isn't it, class? Especially for a couple of boys I know." The class giggles. Then she says, "Nick and Derek, I'd like you to finish your work when you have some free time after lunch." The two boys nod their heads to indicate that they will.

Assigned to groups of three, Ms. Wyatt's students have been working on their papier-mâché relief maps of North America for most of the afternoon. But one group— Molly, Helen, and Lori—has been so busy talking about their favorite television show that they have put little effort into completing their map.

"Hey, you guys," Molly urges, "we'd better get busy. We only have 20 more minutes before we have to go to music."

"Ah, don't worry about it," Helen tells her.

"Yeah, we can always finish tomorrow," Lori adds.

Ms. Wyatt flicks the lights to get her students' attention. "Class, I forgot to tell you about the bonus today. The first group to finish its relief map will have 15 minutes of free time this afternoon."

"All *right!*" several of the children shout.

"Why didn't she tell us earlier?" Helen whispers to her friends.

"It drives me crazy when she does stuff like that," Lori whispers back. "I mean, we could have worked harder if we'd known there was a reason to get done on time."

A bit later, Ms. Wyatt says, "OK, class, it's time to put your relief maps on the back table to dry. As you all know by now, Meesha's group finished its map first, so that group has earned the free time I promised." The class politely claps for Meesha's group.

"Ms. Wyatt, we didn't get our map done," Molly calls out.

"That's 'cause you guys were too busy gossiping," Samantha teases.

"Samantha, it's not nice to tease your classmates," Ms. Wyatt says firmly. She then turns to the three procrastinators. "But girls, I'm not particularly sympathetic.

When I give you an assignment, I expect you to do it. I want the three of you to stay here until you finish it."

"But we'll miss music," whines Helen.

"You should have thought about that before you decided to goof off during your group time."

"Derek and Nicholas got extra time to finish their work this morning," Molly points out.

"Yeah, it isn't fair if they get extra time to complete their work and we don't," Helen adds.

"I don't have any extra time to give you," counters Ms. Wyatt.

"Then why does Meesha's group get extra free time at the end of the day?" Lori asks.

"Enough!" states Ms. Wyatt emphatically. "The rest of you line up for music."

Molly, Helen, and Lori are just finishing their relief map as their classmates return from music class. As soon as all students have settled in their seats, Ms. Wyatt assigns two pages of division problems. "You have 20 minutes to complete these problems before the final bell rings," she announces.

"Ms. Wyatt?" Meesha asks. "What about the free time our group earned earlier? The rule is that free time must be used the same day we earn it. If we don't use it now, then we'll lose it."

"If you want to take the problems home and do them, you certainly can. Otherwise, you should do them in class during your free time."

"How is it free time if we still have to do work?" Meesha persists.

"Meesha, there's only so much time in a day. You can do the problems at home or at school, but you still have to do the problems."

"Last week you let Mary skip an assignment when she earned free time," Meesha reminds her.

"That was *last* week," Ms. Wyatt replies. "I'm sorry that you feel cheated, but you *do* have a choice here. We have a math test scheduled for tomorrow, and some of you need the extra practice with your long division. If you want to waste class time whining, that's your choice too."

Questions for "Consequences"

1. *What inconsistencies do you see in how Ms. Wyatt responds to her students' behavior?*

2. *What might be Ms. Wyatt's rationale for offering free time to the group that finishes its map first?*

3. *Is the free time incentive an effective one?*

4. *In which of the following examples does vicarious reinforcement probably occur, at least for the short run?*
    a. *When Ms. Wyatt makes Molly, Helen, and Lori miss music to finish their project*
    b. *When Ms. Wyatt flicks the lights and tells the students about a bonus for finishing first*
    c. *When Molly, Helen, and Lori don't finish their relief maps because they've been talking*
    d. *When Ms. Wyatt tells the class that Meesha's group has earned free time for finishing first*
5. *On what other occasions might Ms. Wyatt be vicariously reinforcing students?*
6. *Draw from social cognitive theory to explain how Ms. Wyatt eventually punishes Meesha's group.*
7. *Ms. Wyatt doesn't allow Molly's group to attend music class. What message might this action send about music?*
8. *Ms. Wyatt teases Nick and Derek about their budding interest in the opposite sex. Is it appropriate for teachers to tease students in this way? Why or why not?*
9. *How might Ms. Wyatt's inconsistent behavior be affecting the overall psychological climate of the classroom?*

CASE 21
Keeping Track of Business

It's not unusual for students to have trouble adjusting to junior high school, so Ms. Cecere typically waits a couple of months after each new school year has started before contacting parents whose children are struggling in her classes. But she makes an exception in Nathan's case when she sees just how much difficulty he has from the very first day. Concerned about Nathan's progress, she arranges a meeting with Nathan and his parents, Mr. and Ms. Hamlin, one afternoon in early October.

Beginning the meeting, Ms. Cecere says, "I'm worried about how Nathan is doing in my German class. He has yet to turn in a test or quiz completed from start to finish—he usually leaves at least half of the items blank. It puzzles me, though. He almost always gets the questions that he *does* answer correct. And when I ask him about questions that he hasn't responded to, he seems to know the answers to them well enough."

"Sometimes I forget to finish my tests," Nathan explains. "I get distracted a lot."

"I'm like that, too," Mr. Hamlin observes. "I start thinking about other things and lose track of what I'm doing. Like father, like son, I suppose."

"I'm seeing a similar pattern in Nathan's other work," Ms. Cecere continues. "For example, he rarely completes the written exercises that I give in class each day. And when I look at my grade book, I see that Nathan hasn't turned in a single homework assignment all year."

"That surprises me," Ms. Hamlin says. "I make sure that Nathan works on his homework every night. In fact, last night I helped him conjugate the three new verbs you assigned yesterday."

"Well, Nathan didn't turn that assignment in today," Ms. Cecere replies. Mr. and Ms. Hamlin look questioningly at their son.

"I thought I handed it in," he tells them, "but I guess not."

"Nathan, I know you are a bright young man, because you always seem to have the right answer when I call on you. So I'm at a loss to explain why you're not getting your work done."

Mr. Hamlin pauses, seemingly gathering his thoughts together, and then speaks. "I think we should probably tell you, Ms. Cecere, that when Nathan was in second grade, he was diagnosed as having a learning disability. He received special services in his elementary school's resource room for several years after that. But he seems to have licked a lot of the problems he had then. His mother and I would really like him to stay in your class."

Ms. Hamlin pats her son on the knee and adds, "I agree. I don't want him in any more resource rooms."

"Oh, I certainly don't want to get rid of Nathan," Ms. Cecere assures both parents. "On the contrary, I set up this meeting thinking that by putting our heads together, we might identify some strategies to help Nathan be more successful in my class. You said that Nathan received special services when he was in elementary school. What kinds of things seemed to work for him then?"

Ms. Hamlin opens her mouth to reply, but Nathan interrupts. "The doctor put me on drugs because the teachers said I was hyperactive. The drugs made me sleepy all the time. No more drugs!"

"We agree with you on that point," Ms. Hamlin responds. "There won't be any more drugs."

"What things did your resource room teacher do to help you with your school-work, Nathan?" Ms. Cecere asks.

"Well, let's see. Mostly he helped me with my reading. We worked on spelling a lot, and we worked on math some of the time. That's about it."

"I see. Did your teacher ever give you any suggestions to help you make sure you get your work done every day?"

"Not really, no."

Ms. Cecere thinks for a moment. "Well, I think our best bet right now is to identify some ways to make sure that you *do* get your work done. For starters, let's have you use a small notebook to keep track of what assignments your teachers have given you and when each one is due."

Ms. Hamlin pulls such a notebook out of her purse. "Here's one I bought this morning for my grocery lists. Why don't you use it for your assignments, Nathan? I can always get another one for myself."

"It's perfect for what we need," Ms. Cecere observes. "Thank you, Ms. Hamlin. Now let's make three columns on the first page." Ms. Cecere draws two lines down the page and labels the three columns "Assignment," "Due Date," and "Done." "I'd like you to write tonight's assignment—doing the exercise on page 58 of your textbook—in the first column under 'Assignment.' "

After Nathan does so, Ms. Cecere continues, "Good. Now the next thing is to write the assignment's due date, which, in this case, is tomorrow, October 9th. Yes, just like that. You can use the notebook for your other classes too, not just for German. Each night when you sit down to do your homework, use it to remind yourself about what you need to do. Every time you complete an assignment, double-check it to be sure that you have done *everything* that your teacher has asked you to do. Then put a checkmark beside the assignment in the 'Done' column. Finally, when you turn in your work, but *only* when you turn in your work, you can pull out your notebook again and cross out the assignment altogether, because then you know you don't have to worry about it anymore."

"I wonder if maybe either Alice or I should also check Nathan's homework to make sure he hasn't left anything out," Mr. Hamlin offers.

"That's probably a good idea, especially until Nathan gets the hang of this new way of doing things."

"But what about when I'm doing assignments and stuff in class?" Nathan asks.

"I think you told me the other day that Forrest is in your German class, Nathan," Ms. Hamlin says to her son. "He's been your best friend since second grade. Maybe he wouldn't mind looking over your work. Would that be all right with you, Ms. Cecere?"

Ms. Cecere nods and then looks at Nathan. "What do you think of your mom's idea?"

"Yeah, sure. Forrest would probably do anything to keep me in the same class with him." The group laughs. "I might feel a little weird about it, though. Maybe if I can do this notebook thing by myself, then I won't have to have him help me too much."

"Fair enough. Now what can we do about your quizzes and tests?" Ms. Cecere asks.

"I'll recheck each one to make sure that I've answered all the questions. That's something I've never done before. As a matter of fact, I think I'll check it at least twice before I turn it in to you."

"That's a good start, Nathan. And how would you feel if you and I met for a couple of minutes after every class in which you had a quiz or test? That way, I can look over your work with you before I grade it."

"Yeah, that'd be OK. But there's something else. If it's not asking too much, I'd really like to sit at the front of the room. It's hard for me to concentrate when I see everybody doing other stuff in front of me. All I can think about is Freddie blowing his nose or Sheri passing notes. I guess I really need just to think about *German*."

"That's very perceptive of you, Nathan," Ms. Cecere commends him. "Forrest sits in the front row, so why don't you move up next to him. He's a good student, so I know he'll be able to keep you on-task if anyone can."

Three weeks after the meeting, Nathan's work habits have clearly improved. With the help of his notebook, his parents, his friend Forrest, and Ms. Cecere, he is regularly completing both his homework and his in-class assignments. But even the littlest classroom noises—a tapping pencil, a cough, the sound of someone using an eraser—still distract him during quizzes and tests. Ms. Cecere finds a quiet room down the hall where Nathan can take his quizzes and tests undisturbed, and his performance improves considerably. By the end of the semester, Nathan has earned a B in German, and he vows to Forrest that he can surely get an A in spring semester.

Note: Nathan graduated from high school and at last account had a steady job with a large manufacturing company.

Questions for "Keeping Track of Business"

1. *What classic symptoms of a learning disability does Nathan exhibit?*
2. *In what ways does Ms. Cecere accommodate Nathan's special educational needs?*

3.   *Which practice suggested by Ms. Cecere is most consistent with principles of*
      self-regulated learning?
      a. Asking that Forrest look over Nathan's work
      b. Meeting with Nathan after each test and quiz
      c. Encouraging Nathan to keep a notebook for assignments
      d. Involving Nathan's parents in a discussion of how to help him improve his
      classroom performance
4.   *Judging from how Ms. Cecere assesses her students' achievement, both*
      formally and informally, infer her view of what "high achievement" is in her
      class.
5.   *What other strategies might you use to assess students' achievement in a*
      foreign language class?
6.   *What effective strategies does Ms. Cecere use during the meeting?*

CASE 22
Solving Problems

Ms. Fieseler doesn't want her eighth-grade prealgebra students just to memorize the mathematical procedures she teaches them; she also wants them to be able to use those procedures to solve actual problems. So she frequently assigns word problems related to whatever topics are currently under discussion. In Ms. Fieseler's mind, the problems she assigns are pretty straightforward and sometimes downright obvious. Yet many of her students have difficulty solving them independently. Thinking they might be more successful if they work together, she decides to incorporate the problems into a cooperative group activity at the end of each week.

Today, Ms. Fieseler has instructed the cooperative groups to solve the following three problems:

> Your parents have given you permission to redecorate your bedroom. You want to build a shelf for your books on the wall beside your bed. The wall is 15 feet across. Your dad has given you a lot of metal shelf brackets and some pieces of wood that are each 18 inches long, 6 inches wide, and 1 inch thick. How many pieces of wood will you need if you want to make one long shelf that goes across the entire wall?

> Now you want to paint your bedroom. The paint comes in 1-gallon cans, and paint from a single can will cover 200–250 square feet. If your bedroom is 15 feet long and 10 feet wide, and if your ceiling is 8 feet from the floor, how many cans of paint will you need?

> You also want to lay new carpet in your bedroom. It costs $9 a square yard. How much will you need to buy carpet that covers the entire floor?

"Now remember, class," Ms. Fieseler tells her students, "your performance on all of your group problem-solving exercises this semester will be worth one-third of your final class grade. You need to work together to make sure everyone in your group understands what he or she is doing."

One group sitting in the far corner of the room includes four students—Jack, Leo, Elizabeth, and Olivia—who are highly motivated to do well on the assignment. The fifth group member, Seth, would rather be playing video games on the portable Nintendo hidden in his backpack than work on math problems with classmates he perceives as "nerds."

"You're late, Seth," Elizabeth admonishes him as he approaches the table. "And get those pencils out of your nose. That is *soooo* gross!"

Leo and Olivia laugh at the walrus-like image Seth has created by sticking two pencils up his nostrils. Seth grins and then transplants the pencils to his ears. Olivia rolls her eyes; the other three group members ignore his childish behavior.

"We're on the second problem already, Seth," Leo says. "This one's about painting, and it's really hard. Your dad's a painter, isn't he? Come on, tell us what we should do."

Seth glances at the problem Olivia is pointing to, then impulsively writes "101" in the margin beside it.

"Seth! What are you doing?!" Jack asks indignantly. "You just made the answer up, didn't you?"

"He has to be faking it," Elizabeth points out. "There's no way the answer can be so high."

"One hundred and one Dalmatians," Seth explains. "Get it?"

"What do Dalmatians have to do with the problem?" Leo asks. "Grow up, Seth."

"Geez, you guys got no sense of humor," Seth responds. "Who cares about this stuff anyway?"

"Seth, don't you care about your grades?" Elizabeth asks. "Even if *you* don't care, your parents probably do."

"Yeah, right! My folks don't give as s--- how I do in school. They'd think I was great even if I was robbing banks."

"You guys, we need to get back to work," Leo reminds the group.

Seth scrawls "29" next to the third problem. Ignoring him, the other four students discuss the second problem at length and eventually reach the correct answer of "2 cans." They then struggle with the third problem but eventually conclude that they don't have all the information they need to solve the problem. At the end of the group session, the group turns in a sheet of paper that lists all five group members and solutions to the first two problems.

"Ms. Fieseler, I'm getting tired of the same people doing all the work when we're in groups," Jack complains.

"Yeah, it isn't fair," Elizabeth adds. "Only a few of us do the work, yet everyone gets credit."

"So what do you think we should do about the situation?" Ms. Fieseler asks.

The students expect their teacher to answer her own question, but she remains silent. Finally Olivia proposes a solution. "I say we kick any goof-offs out of the group."

"Hmm," Ms. Fieseler responds pensively, "is that what people in the business world do?"

"Absolutely!" says Leo. "They fire anyone who's too lazy to help out. I think we should do the same thing—you know, 'fire' lazy people from our groups. They can do their *own* work."

"Sometimes people are stuck with one another," Linda points out from across the room. "Like, my mom has to work with this jerk who doesn't do anything except sit around and look smart all day. She's always complaining at home about how she has to pick up the slack."

"Linda's right," Ms. Fieseler tells the class. "You're basically stuck with one another in your cooperative groups. So how can we make sure that everyone participates constructively during group time?"

"I say we don't speak to anyone who *doesn't* help out," Mary suggests.

"Maybe when we turn in the answer sheets we fill out, we should only let the people who have worked enough on the problems sign their names," Elizabeth says.

"Hmm . . . how will we know what 'enough work' is?" Ms. Fieseler asks.

"If someone tries to help at least once, then that person is contributing to the group," Mary answers.

"But how would you decide that the person has actually *contributed?*" Ms. Fieseler asks.

"Well, you know, if they seem like they're trying real hard, even if they're wrong, they're contributing," Joe volunteers. "And especially if they try to explain the steps they went through to solve the problem, then they're contributing."

"But what if somebody absolutely refuses to help out?" Leo calls out.

"Then they don't get the group reward," states Ms. Fieseler. "Remember, the group with the most points at the end of the month doesn't have to do any homework for a week."

Questions for "Solving Problems"

1. *Many math teachers use word problems to help students transfer mathematical concepts and procedures to real-world contexts. Do you think word problems are an effective way of doing that? Why or why not?*
2. *Leo and Olivia laugh when Seth puts two pencils up his nose, but none of the group members laugh when he puts the pencils in his ears. Which one of the following concepts from behaviorism best describes what has occurred in the group?*
    a. Generalization
    b. Primary reinforcement
    c. Vicarious reinforcement
    d. Intermittent reinforcement
3. *Why does Seth's group conclude that it doesn't have all the information it needs to solve the third problem?*
4. *Which one of the following cognitive factors is most likely to be hindering Seth's group from solving the third problem?*
    a. Limited working memory capacity
    b. Incorrect encoding of the problem
    c. Nonretrieval of relevant prior knowledge
    d. Inappropriate attributions to an external cause
5. *What are the potential benefits of assigning cooperative group activities as a way of helping the students learn how to solve challenging word problems?*
6. *Why do you think Seth is not participating productively in the group task?*
7. *There will often be students who, like Seth, hope to get a "free ride" during cooperative group time. Does Ms. Fieseler resolve the "free rider" situation?*
8. *How might Ms. Fieseler encourage Seth to participate in the cooperative learning activity?*
9. *At the end of the case study, Ms. Fieseler tells her students, "The group with the most points at the end of the month doesn't have to do any homework for a week." Is this a good idea? Why or why not?*

10. *Members of Seth's group complain that they are at a disadvantage in earning the group reward because one of its members (Seth) refuses to do any work. If **only** this group has such a disadvantage, then Ms. Fieseler's strategy is lacking which important quality of a good assessment?*
    a. *Validity*
    b. *Reliability*
    c. *Practicality*
    d. *Standardization*

11. *Ms. Fieseler informs her students that their performance on the group problem-solving exercises is worth one-third of their final grade. Is this an appropriate assessment practice? Why or why not?*

CASE 23
First Aid

The students in Mr. Mandabach's eighth-grade health class seem to be more hyperactive than usual this morning. Mr. Mandabach loudly clears his throat as a way of getting their attention. "All right, class," he says, "let's get started." He pauses until everyone has settled down. Out of the corner of his eye, he sees Ruth and Marisa quickly exchanging notes.

"As you know, we've been studying first aid procedures for a couple of weeks. Today we're going to learn how we can help someone who has been in a serious accident." As Mr. Mandabach is speaking, he sees Paul pass a note to JoAnn.

Suddenly Mr. Mandabach remembers that the spring dance is coming up in a few days. Based on his 5 years' experience at Montview Junior High, he expects that the frequency of note passing among his young adolescents will increase considerably between now and then. In his first year of teaching at Montview, he always confiscated any notes he saw and kept the culprits after class. But he eventually stopped the practice after a girl burst into tears as he read her note aloud to the others. So today he simply ignores any note passing he sees and continues with his lesson.

"Now imagine that you're all by yourself and come across an accident victim who is obviously unconscious. What do you think you should check first—breathing, airway, or circulation?"

"Airway," says Marie. Behind Marie, Juanita is shoving a note under Vicki's textbook.

"No—circulation," says Gary, "because people can bleed to death in a matter of minutes."

"It's breathing!" Ryan shouts. "If people don't get enough oxygen to their brains, they can become mentally retarded. People can even *die* if they don't get enough oxygen. Right, Mr. M.?"

"Yes," Mr. Mandabach agrees, "as you know, people can die if they go without oxygen for very long. Even if they *don't* die, they may suffer permanent brain damage."

"See, I told you, man!" exclaims Ryan.

"But now imagine this situation," Mr. Mandabach says. "A woman is eating a donut while she's driving to work one day. To help wash down the donut, she reaches for a can of Coke that's sitting in a cup holder next to her. As she does so, she takes her eyes off the road for a split second and crashes her car into a tree. She's not wearing a seat belt, so she's thrown 50 feet from the vehicle. You're riding your bike to school when you see the accident, and so you rush over to see what you can do to help. The woman is unconscious, and you see blood seeping from under her shirt. What should you do?"

"I'd call 911 on her cell phone and wait for help to arrive," Greg replies.

"I'd lecture her about her poor eating habits!" Malcolm jokes.

Mr. Mandabach is pleased to see that all eyes are on him and the note passing has finally stopped. He repeats his question: "What would you *really* do to help?"

"Well, I'd look under her shirt to see where the blood is coming from," says Melody. "If she's bleeding a lot, then I'd apply pressure to the wound with my hand. I'd put my jacket between the wound and my hand, though, so I wouldn't get any of her blood on me."

"That's a good suggestion, Melody." Mr. Mandabach replies. "But how do you know if she's breathing? Maybe the bleeding is really a very minor problem compared to other things that are wrong."

Samantha raises her hand, and Mr. Mandabach nods his permission for her to speak. "Put your ear by her mouth and nose to see if you can feel her breath. Look at her chest so you can tell if it's rising or not."

"Aha!" Mr. Mandabach responds. "So what do you do if you see that she's *not* breathing? Think about what we did with the mannequins last week when the person from the Red Cross came to visit."

"Do CPR!" yells most of the class.

"Wait a minute," says Marie. "How do we know she's not choking on the donut? Maybe it's blocking her airway."

Mr. Mandabach looks around the room for reactions to Marie's observation, but there are none. "This time we *know* the person was eating prior to the accident. But most of the time we aren't so lucky. We may not have a clue about what's going on when we first see an injured person. We should always check an unconscious person's *airway* first. Why do you think we should do this?"

"Because if we did CPR and her airway was blocked, we wouldn't be doing her any good," Gary replies.

"Right! You wouldn't be able to get any oxygen to her lungs no matter *what* you did. But now say that her airway *isn't* blocked. What would you do then?"

"You'd give her CPR," Malcolm answers.

"Right again," says Mr. Mandabach. "So . . . *airway, breathing,* and then what?"

"Circulation," Greg says.

"Good," says Mr. Mandabach. "We treat someone's bleeding—we deal with *circulation* problems—only after we've already made sure that he or she is breathing."

"Mr. M.?" asks Alisa. "What if we're all stressed out and can't remember which one comes first?"

"You have a point, Alisa," Mr. Mandabach responds. "But fortunately someone from the Red Cross came up with a very simple way to remember the order of first aid responses: *A-B-C* for *airway, breathing, circulation.*"

"That's pretty clever the way you used A-B-C, Mr. M.," Blake tells him.

"Isn't it, though? OK, now let's consider another situation . . . "

Questions for "First Aid"

1. *In which of the following instances does Mr. Mandabach clearly show **withitness**?*
    a. He sees Ruth and Marisa passing notes.
    b. He encourages Malcolm to expand on his answer.
    c. He realizes that a school dance is coming up soon.
    d. He provides practical examples to encourage meaningful learning.

2. *Early in his teaching career, Mr. Mandabach always confiscated any notes he saw students passing in class. But now he usually ignores such note passing. Does his change reflect sound teaching practice? Why or why not?*

3. *What would you do if students were passing notes during a lesson?*

4. *How does Mr. Mandabach finally focus his students' attention on the topic of first aid?*

5. *Examine Mr. Mandabach's teaching practices during the lesson. Do they encourage rote learning or meaningful learning? Support your answer with two or more specific strategies from the case.*

6. ***Lower-level questions*** *require students to recall information in essentially the same form that they initially learned it.* ***Higher-level questions*** *require students to do something new with what they've learned—perhaps analyzing it, integrating it, or applying it. What types of questions does Mr. Mandabach ask?*

7. ***Retrieval cues*** *are hints that help students recall previously learned information from long-term memory. On what two occasions does Mr. Mandabach give his students retrieval cues to help them remember things they've previously learned?*

8. *Mr. Mandabach introduces the mnemonic "A-B-C" as a simple way for students to remember the order of first aid responses:* ***airway, breathing, circulation.*** *Which one of the following terms best describes the mnemonic technique he is encouraging his students to use?*
   a. *Keyword method*
   b. *Verbal mediation*
   c. *Distributed cognition*
   d. *Superimposed meaningful structure*

9. *What evidence do you see that students are constructing new understandings in response to Mr. Mandabach's questions rather than simply retrieving the responses from long-term memory?*

10. *How frequently does Mr. Mandabach give students feedback about their responses?*

11. *From Piaget's perspective, at what stage of cognitive development must students be in order to understand this lesson?*

12. *In Vygotsky's theory, the zone of proximal development (ZPD) is the range of tasks that a student can perform only with the assistance of a more capable individual. Is Mr. Mandabach teaching within students' ZPD?*

CASE 24
The Respiratory System

Ms. McNaught has recently acquired some computer software she can use to teach human anatomy and physiology to her high school biology students. The software depicts three-dimensional models of the human body that simulate such physiological phenomena as circulation, respiration, and digestion. The software also allows students to explore the models in a variety of ways—for example, by rotating or magnifying them, isolating particular systems or organs for closer inspection, or running simulations of specific systems.

Today Ms. McNaught's students are in the computer lab using the new software to examine the "ins" and "outs" of human respiration. Sitting in pairs at computer terminals around the room, the students have been instructed to identify the various components of the respiratory system, determine the function of each component, and explain how everything works in harmony to make respiration possible. Ms. McNaught gives each pair of students a worksheet on which to record observations and answer specific questions and then moves around the room to monitor students' progress and provide assistance where necessary. As she circulates, she hears snippets of several conversations.

Beau, a computer wiz, is the first student to bring a model of the respiratory system up on the computer screen. "OK, Joan," he instructs his partner, "list these parts of the respiratory system: trachea, lungs, bronchi, bronchioles." He points to each part of the model as he names it, and Joan dutifully records the terms on the worksheet. Then Beau moves the mouse and clicks on another part of the screen. "Now let's see if we can make this guy breathe . . . "

As Ms. McNaught moves away from Beau and Joan, she overhears what Russell is saying to his partner Sally: "Put the names of the lobes here. No, not down there. Look at the computer model. This here is the middle lobe. This part down here is called the lower lobe."

Sally erases what she's written and then writes "middle lobe" and "lower lobe" in the places where Russell has indicated.

"What does it say to do next?" Russell asks.

"Ah . . . let's see. Oh, now we're supposed to figure out what the diaphragm and the rib cage do during respiration."

From another direction, Ms. McNaught overhears Carol complaining to her partner Keith. "Quit moving the model so fast. Honestly, I have to tell you this every time we do labs together! You change what's on the computer screen so fast that I can't get everything down on the worksheet. Come on, stop playing around, and turn the screen a little bit so I can at least see some of it."

The following day, Ms. McNaught conducts a class discussion of the respiratory system. "So who can tell me . . . what do the diaphragm and rib cage do when we breathe?"

"The diaphragm moves down and the rib cage moves out," Diana answers.

"That's right. The diaphragm is a dome-shaped muscle just below the lungs, and when we breathe, it tightens and moves downward. At the same time, the muscles between the ribs pull the rib cage upward and outward. Now which process are we talking about here—inhaling or exhaling?"

"Inhaling," Keith answers.

"Good. Can you explain why you know it's inhaling?"

"Well, the diaphragm flattens out, and the rib cage moves forward, so there's more room inside the chest, and so air can come in."

"Good job, Keith. So what happens when the air enters the chest?"

After referring to his notes, Mark answers, "Air goes through the trachea and then through the bronchioles and into the alveoli."

"What happens when the air gets to the alveoli, Mark?" Ms. McNaught asks.

"Well, the alveoli are surrounded by lots of little blood vessels. The oxygen in the air passes through the membranes between the alveoli and the blood vessels and then goes into the blood."

"Excellent. Now which muscle does most of the work when we breathe?"

"The diaphragm," Kathy responds.

"Right," says Ms. McNaught. "About how many times a minute does a typical adult inhale and exhale?"

"About 10 to 16 times," Oliver replies.

"Is that when we're resting or working hard?"

"When we're resting," Martin responds. "It's faster when we're running or something."

"Very good! OK, class, for your homework assignment this weekend, I'd like you to write a one-page essay describing how the respiratory system works in conjunction with the cardiovascular system. In doing so, I hope you'll begin to realize just what marvelous machines our bodies really are. Class dismissed."

Questions for "The Respiratory System"

1. *How might a computer simulation facilitate students' ability to construct an understanding of physiological systems?*
2. *Do you think that computer software that provides models and simulations of real-life systems and events can reasonably replace actual physical objects in high school science courses?*
3. *Ms. McNaught ignores the students' bickering during their laboratory time. Is this a good strategy? Why or why not?*
4. *Which one of the following questions is the best example of a **higher-level question**?*
   a. *"So who can tell me . . . what do the diaphragm and rib cage do when we breathe?"*
   b. *"Now which process are we talking about here—inhaling or exhaling?"*

     c. "Can you explain why you know it's inhaling?"
     d. "Which muscle does most of the work when we breathe?"

5. *Identify specific examples of how Ms. McNaught expands on her students' answers. Explain how doing so may facilitate students' learning.*

6. *In what ways are the male and female students in Ms. McNaught's class having different educational experiences?*

7. *Under the circumstances, why are the male students likely to learn and remember more than the female students about how the human respiratory system works?*

8. *Like most teachers, Ms. McNaught probably has no idea that her female students are having a different educational experience from the males. As a teacher, how might you minimize gender bias in your classroom?*

CASE 25
The Concept Maps

Seventeen-year-old Robin is determined to be ready if her teacher, Mr. Kessinger, calls on her during her third-period world history class. Last night she prepared a concept map—a diagram that depicts important interrelationships among the concepts in a chapter or unit—to help her remember the events that eventually led the United States to join the Allied Forces during World War II. Now she has both her concept map and her notebook lying in front of her on her desk. As Mr. Kessinger fires questions at his class, Robin writes her classmates' responses in her notebook.

"So, Jacob, why didn't the United States jump in and help the Europeans when World War II began?"

"Well, at the beginning of the war, we thought the people in Europe should handle their own battles. When we first heard about how Hitler was having lots of Jewish people killed, we didn't believe that anybody could do such a thing. We thought all the stories were just lies that the media made up."

"Micki, when did we finally realize there were many concentration camps in Europe?"

"Uh . . . I'm not sure exactly," Micki answers hesitantly.

"Well, you should be!" Mr. Kessinger angrily admonishes her.

Micki squirms in her seat, then attempts to answer her teacher's question. "Well . . . when people . . . um . . . when European news reporters started sending us pictures of how horrible the war was, then we started getting involved. We . . . um . . . "

"I think that starting tonight, Micki, you'd better read your history book a little more carefully. Robin, what event brought the United States into World War II?"

Taking a look at her concept map, Robin begins, "It was . . . " But then she sees Mr. Kessinger towering over her desk.

"What??!! You're using *notes??!!*" he screams as he tears her concept map into shreds.

As she watches the pieces of paper fall to the floor, she thinks to herself, "I worked for more than an hour on that concept map. Kessinger had no right to tear it up." Her teacher is saying something to her, but she doesn't hear him.

"Well, Robin? I'm waiting for an answer! What gives you the right to cheat in my class?!!" The rest of the class is quiet; everyone is too stunned to speak.

"I . . . I didn't think I was cheating," Robin stammers. "It's not as if this was a test. I thought I was supposed to be in here to learn. My concept maps help me connect different ideas together."

"You are expected to know this stuff before you come to class. If you ever pull such a stunt again, I will insist that you drop my class. Do I make myself *clear?!*"

Robin doesn't answer. And she doesn't look up from her desk until the bell rings. Her notebook remains open in front of her, but she writes nothing else in it for the rest of the class period.

❖❖❖

Later in the day, as Robin is walking down the hall to Ms. Yamashita's psychology class, Jane and Cami run to catch up with her.

"Hey, are you OK, Robin?" Jane asks her. "I can't believe what Old Man Kessinger did to you today."

"I just hate him. I really do," Cami adds. "I mean, who cares if we take notes?"

As the three friends continue complaining about their world history teacher, they hear the bell ring. They hurry to their psychology class, arriving after class has already begun. Robin slips into her seat in the front row, pulls her psychology notebook out of her backpack, and opens it to the notes she wrote from her assigned readings the night before.

"Nice of you girls to join us," Ms. Yamashita says, smiling. "We're talking about Freud. Robin, what did Freud mean when he talked about the *id?*"

"The *id* is . . . uh . . . " As Robin pauses, she looks down at her notebook and realizes that the concept map she drew of Freud's theory is in full view of her teacher. Before she has a chance to hide it, Ms. Yamashita is at Robin's desk and looking at her work. Robin cringes, expecting the worst.

"Why, Robin! This is lovely! Do you mind if I copy it for everyone else? Class, you should see this beautiful concept map that Robin has created."

Oblivious to what her teacher is saying, Robin jumps quickly out of her seat and runs down the hall to the restroom, crying and shaking uncontrollably.

Note: Robin never again took notes of any kind in Mr. Kessinger's class.

Questions for "The Concept Maps"

1. *Which one of the following principles of classroom management did Mr. Kessinger most clearly violate?*
   a. *Create a warm, respectful classroom climate.*
   b. *Give students some control over classroom activities.*
   c. *Communicate appropriate messages about school subject matter.*
   d. *Include students in decision making about classroom procedures.*
2. *Psychologists often distinguish between two general kinds of punishment:* **presentation punishment** *(in which an aversive stimulus is presented after a response) and* **removal punishment** *(in which a desired stimulus is taken away after a response). Which kind of punishment does Mr. Kessinger give Robin?*
3. *Explain Robin's reaction in Ms. Yamashita's class from the perspective of classical conditioning.*
4. *What possible benefits might concept maps have?*
5. *What important role do Jane and Cami play in the events that transpire?*

CASE 26
Coming Back to School

Wesley Karasov was a top student at West Hills High School until last year, when he sustained a serious head injury in a motorcycle accident. He has undergone months of rehabilitation since the accident, and his parents and rehabilitation therapists believe that he is now ready to return to school. Today Wesley and his parents are meeting in the school conference room with Wesley's former teachers, Principal Roz Wiggins, and Ms. Gila Seaver, the school's special education teacher. As a group, they will decide on an appropriate placement for Wesley.

After welcoming everyone to the meeting, Principal Wiggins begins the discussion. "Frankly, I'm not sure he is ready to come back to school at all. I have the report from the psychologist at the rehab center, and it looks as if his test scores just aren't where they need to be, especially for someone in his senior year of high school. In my mind, the best option right now is a private tutor. The school district has an excellent tutor on its payroll, and she could work with him at home for a couple of hours each afternoon."

As Wesley clears his throat to speak, all eyes turn to look at him. "My name is Wesley," he says in a slow, faltering voice. "I would appreciate it if you call me by my name. I am a person, not some object. It's my senior year, and I *want to come back to school!*"

Wesley's mother, Mrs. Karasov, steps in. "Ms. Wiggins, I'd like to remind you that Wesley has had a traumatic brain injury, something that entitles him to an appropriate education in the least restrictive environment possible. All three of us—Wesley, my husband, and I—have thought and talked a great deal about Wesley's situation, and we all believe quite strongly that his academic needs *can* be met in a regular high school environment. Since the accident, I've learned a lot about traumatic brain injuries—TBI. For instance, I've learned that people with TBI sometimes have rapid, and often quite sudden, improvements in mental capacity. These kids need stimulation, and they need to be challenged."

"If Wesley were to come back to school right now, he'd probably have to spend most of the day in my special education classroom," Ms. Seaver observes. "His test scores are way below grade level. For example, I saw in the psychologist's report that he's reading at a first-grade level now. How can he possibly keep up with his classmates if he can't read high school level textbooks?"

Mrs. Karasov bites her tongue as she tries to keep her temper. "You've been looking at the test scores on *timed* tests, Ms. Seaver. Kids with head injuries usually need more time than other kids to think about what they read. Besides, Wesley took those tests 8 months ago. He's grown a lot—mentally, I mean—since then."

As the principal opens her mouth to respond, Mr. Karasov enters the conversation. "With all due respect, Ms. Wiggins and Ms. Seaver, I think you're both grossly underestimating what Wesley is capable of doing. If you don't mind, I'd like to try a little experiment. I borrowed one of your school's history textbooks from a friend of Wesley's, and I've brought it with me today." Handing the book to the principal, he continues, "Choose any chapter you like, Ms. Wiggins. Then let's send Wesley to the library to read it while we continue our discussion. Is that OK with you, Wesley?"

"I'll do whatever it takes to get me back in school," Wesley responds.

Wesley's parents and the members of the school faculty are in a heated debate when Wesley returns to the conference room with the history book and several sheets of notes. Ms. Wiggins asks Mr. Hermanowitz, Wesley's former history teacher, to quiz Wesley on the chapter's content. Occasionally referring to his notes, Wesley correctly answers every question that Mr. Hermanowitz asks him.

Ms. Wiggins looks at her colleagues, and their agreement about the situation is clear. She turns to Wesley and smiles. "I guess we owe you an apology, Wesley. You definitely *are* ready to come back to school. What can we do to make your life easier here at West Hills High?"

"Well, ma'am," Wesley responds, "I get tired easily. Sometimes I need to take a nap during the day. I forget what to do if I don't write things down. And mostly I just need more time than the other students."

As he attends his classes each day, Wesley keeps meticulous notes about the assignments he needs to complete and the due date for each one; as a result, he's far more diligent than many of his classmates in getting his work done. He takes all of his tests in a room near the main office so that he has time to think about each question carefully; when he spends so much time completing his tests that he's late to other classes, the school secretary sends a note along with him to explain his tardiness.

By the end of second period each day, Wesley is so exhausted that he takes a 2-hour nap on a couch in the nurse's office, but he wakes up refreshed enough to attend two more classes in the afternoon. The only drawback to his routine is that he's had to drop two of the classes he needs to graduate.

Meanwhile, Wesley's teachers are so impressed with the young man's determination to succeed that they bend over backwards to *help* him succeed. Aware of his difficulties in processing information quickly and in remembering what he's read and heard, they make a variety of accommodations on his behalf. For example, Wesley's math teacher assigns him only half of the in-class exercises that she assigns the rest of the class; she asks him to do the remaining exercises at his leisure at home. His English teacher always writes directions to assignments on the board and then states them orally as well. His history teacher signals main ideas by saying, "This is important, so put it in your notes."

Ms. Struthers, Wesley's French teacher, is the most accommodating of all. Wesley had 3 years of French prior to his accident, but he remembers very little of what he used to know so well. Although he's officially enrolled in French IV, Ms. Struthers teaches him out of the French I textbook. She encourages Wesley to speak in French in class, but she's patient when he struggles, and she occasionally gives him a word he needs if he has difficulty remembering it on his own. And whenever she gives her class a quiz, Wesley takes a French I quiz instead.

In a follow-up meeting, Wesley expresses his gratitude that the teachers are being so helpful and supportive. Other than having to give up his third- and fourth-hour classes, he thinks he has made a smooth transition back to school. Ms. Wiggins notes that all of Wesley's teachers are pleased with his progress.

Note: Wesley earned A's in everything except French that semester; however, he finished two courses shy of the school's graduation requirements. The school allowed him to attend his class's graduation ceremony in May but did not award him a diploma until August, after he had completed the missing courses in summer school.

Questions for "Coming Back to School"

1. *What mistakes do Ms. Wiggins and Ms. Seaver make when they interpret the test scores that the psychologist has reported?*
2. *In questioning Ms. Wiggins's and Ms. Seaver's interpretation of Wesley's test scores, which one of the following characteristics of a good assessment instrument is Mrs. Karasov calling into question?*
   a. *Validity*
   b. *Reliability*
   c. *Practicality*
   d. *Standardization*
3. *Wesley's father assures the group that Wesley is capable of doing grade-level work. To demonstrate this point, he asks Wesley to read a chapter in a history book in the school library; upon his return, Mr. Hermanowitz quizzes him on its content. Are the results of this assessment a good indicator of Wesley's ability to do grade-level work? Why or why not?*
4. *As a result of his injuries, Wesley's teachers bend over backwards to help him succeed. Are the accommodations they provide for Wesley fair to the other students at West Hills High School? Why or why not?*
5. *What accommodations do school personnel make for Wesley's disability?*
6. *If you had Wesley in your classroom, what other strategies might you use to help him succeed?*
7. *Vygotsky proposed that cognitive development is most likely to occur when children and adolescents work within their zone of proximal development—that is, when they tackle tasks that they can accomplish only with the help of a more advanced individual. What strategies does the French teacher use to make sure that Wesley is working within his ZPD?*
8. *Should Wesley be officially enrolled in French IV? Why or why not?*
9. *Under the circumstances, should the school waive some of the graduation requirements in Wesley's case? Why or why not?*

CASE 27
Animal Shelters

For a 4-year-old, Sasha has an unusual ability to focus on a single topic or activity for extended periods of time. For instance, when the other children in her preschool class draw a series of pictures in the blank "picture books" that their teachers have created, they are apt to change subject matter with every page—perhaps drawing a house on page 1, a cat on page 2, a tree on page 3, and so on, with no rhyme or reason to the collection. In contrast, Sasha's books all have themes: She makes one that is all flowers, another that is all animals, and a third in which she's drawn pictures of different family members. And when the children dictate stories for their teachers to transcribe, only Sasha's story has a plot line that carries a sequence of events from beginning to end.

Sasha is also a very independent, self-directed young girl. She happily tackles puzzles, art projects, and other hands-on tasks with little or no guidance or assistance from others. In fact, Sasha can be a bit *too* self-directed, in that she resists her teachers' efforts to engage her in preplanned activities. "Sasha doesn't like to be told what to do," one of her teachers, Ms. Bergeron, explains. "Part of the problem is that she gets anxious if she doesn't know exactly what's going to happen in an activity. But she also seems to have a control issue: She wants *herself* to be the one in charge."

The children in Sasha's class spend most of the day in activities they choose themselves—perhaps experimenting at the sand table, constructing houses and forts with Lego blocks, or concocting elaborate scenarios at the "grocery store" or "doctor's office" in the dramatic play area. But the children always have one required task to do at some point or other during the day. The task varies from day to day but is always completed at the Round Table, a large table in the middle of the room. Here the children can find all of the materials they need for the task, and one of their teachers is always close by to provide instructions and offer a helping hand.

Since the beginning of the school year, Sasha has refused to come to the Round Table. Sometimes she will do the required project, but only at another location. For example, when a child has a birthday, every member of the class creates a page for the child's Birthday Book by drawing a picture or writing a simple message. "Sasha will eventually make a page," Ms. Bergeron says, "but she'll do it somewhere else—say, at the reading-writing table in the corner."

One day in January the daily project is to create a shelter for a small animal. The class has been studying shelters—what a *shelter* is, how houses provide shelter for people, what types of shelters woodland creatures use, and so on. The Round Table has a collection of ceramic animal knick-knacks that the teachers have found at home or purchased at neighborhood yard sales; the children are each asked to select an animal for which they would like to build a shelter. In addition, the table has a variety of natural materials for creating shelters, including twigs, larger sticks, pebbles, tree bark, grass, and pine cones. It also has pieces of corrugated cardboard to be used as "ground" on which the shelters can be built, plus glue and rubber bands to help hold the children's creations together.

As usual, Sasha refuses to come to the Round Table. She really loves animals, however, and so she hovers close by and watches the other children at work. Eventually she approaches the table, chooses a rabbit to build a home for, and tentatively begins to work on her shelter. Her teachers say nothing to communicate that she has done anything unusual, but they grin knowingly at one another, as if to say, "Yes! Finally she's done it!"

The children's animal shelters take several days to complete, and each day Sasha willingly approaches the Round Table to work on her rabbit house. And in the weeks that follow, never again does she balk at completing whatever Round Table task is assigned. Because the table can accommodate only a few children at any one time, the teachers often suggest that Sasha be one of the first to work there. Once she's completed the assigned task, she can have the rest of the day to pursue activities of her own choosing without fear of being interrupted.

Questions for "Animal Shelters"

1. Which one of the following principles of human motivation best explains Sasha's "control issue"?
    a. Human beings appear to have a basic need for self-determination.
    b. Children often internalize the standards that adults have for their behavior.
    c. Children are more likely to pursue a task for which they have high self-efficacy.
    d. Situational interest is often evoked by an event that is novel, unusual, or puzzling.
2. When drawing pictures in the blank "picture books," most of Sasha's classmates have trouble sticking to a single theme. Given what you have learned about cognitive development, would you guess that such difficulty is typical or atypical for this age group?
3. What are some possible reasons why Sasha initially resists coming to the Round Table?
4. In the early weeks of the school year, the teachers strongly encourage Sasha to come to the Round Table, but they never **force** her to do so. Is this approach appropriate? Justify your answer.

CASE 28
I Bit My Tongue

The children in Ms. Chang's preschool class often have trouble keeping their emotions in check when they get stressed or upset. But many of them do have strategies they use to help calm themselves down. Some children seek comfort from Ms. Chang or one of the two teacher interns in the classroom. Some children temporarily retreat to a beanbag chair in a quiet corner of the room. Some children retrieve objects—perhaps a teddy bear, pillow, or favorite blanket—that they've brought from home and keep in their personal storage cubbies.

One child, 4-year-old Austin, cries often but is not easily soothed. When Ms. Chang asks him what the matter is, he typically responds, "I bit my tongue." The first two or three times Austin complains of a bitten tongue, Ms. Chang asks him to open his mouth. She can see no damage but acknowledges that tongue bites are not always obvious to an outsider. Yet eventually she begins to suspect that Austin's tongue is seldom if ever the true source of his distress.

As Ms. Chang observes Austin more closely over the next few weeks, she discovers that he cries every time he is frustrated in assigned tasks or slighted in his interactions with peers, and so she takes a new approach in responding to his tears. For example, on one occasion, several children are playing "doctor" in the dramatic play area. Because Austin's parents are both physicians, he wants to join the group as a "surgeon." However, Ms. Chang has previously decreed that only four children can play in the drama area at a time, and the scenario under way already has a doctor (Niesha), a nurse (Annie), and two patients (Weston and Lucy). Austin bursts into tears and as usual claims to have bitten his tongue. Ms. Chang gently takes him aside and says, "I see that the drama area is full right now. But I know that Lucy has to leave for a *real* doctor's appointment in a few minutes, and then there will be room for you to join the group. Why don't you and I find something else for you to do while you wait? Aha, here's Richard Scarry's *Best Storybook Ever!* I know this is one of your favorites. How about if I read one of the stories to you? By the time I'm done, I bet the hospital will be ready for a new surgeon."

Questions for "I Bit My Tongue"

1. *Children vary considerably in their ability to restrain their behaviors when they have a strong emotional reaction to an event. Such restraint is an example of which one of the following?*
    a. *Skinner's concept of* **shaping**
    b. *Piaget's concept of* **assimilation**
    c. *Bandura's concept of* **self-regulation**
    d. *Vygotsky's concept of* **internalization**
2. *If you were a preschool teacher, would you allow children to bring objects of comfort from home? Why or why not?*

3.   *Why does Austin say, "I bit my tongue"?*
4.   *Why does Ms. Chang limit the number of children who can be at the dramatic play area at once? What are the advantages of dramatic play for young children?*
5.   *Would you have handled Austin's response to the "doctor" situation as Ms. Chang did? Why or why not?*

CASE 29
Letters

After Ms. Bernstein's kindergartners arrive at their classroom the first thing Monday morning, they quickly put their backpacks and other items from home in their tote trays. They then go straight to the front of the room, find an empty spot on the painted red circle on the floor, and listen to the story that Ms. Bernstein is already starting to read aloud. School always begins with an exciting story, and the children don't want to miss it by squandering their time at their tote trays.

After she finishes the story, Ms. Bernstein sings hello to everyone by name to the tune of "Happy Birthday," like so:

> Good morning to Jack.
> Good morning to Jack.
> How are you this morning?

At this point, the child who's been identified in the song sings the final line:

> I'm fine, how are you?

The children are always delighted when they hear their own names called out in the song; their names are a signal that they, too, can sing along with Ms. Bernstein. Once everyone has joined in, Ms. Bernstein brings the song to a close.

"Who *wasn't* in our song today?" she asks.

"Antonio wasn't in the song, Ms. Bernstein," Margaret calls out. "Remember? He has a doctor's appointment this morning."

"Denzel's not here, either," adds Justin. "He still has the flu."

Ms. Bernstein writes "Antonio" and "Denzel" on the chalkboard, sounding out each letter as she writes it. "So . . . we have Antonio and Denzel absent today. Let's see, this week's office helper is Jon. Will you take this absentee form to the office for us, Jon?"

As Jon leaves the room, Ms. Bernstein begins a game of Riddly Riddly Ree, a game that the children know well: "Riddly riddly ree, I see something you don't see. It has the colors red, white, and blue. It begins with the letter F. What is it?"

"The fan!" responds Lena.

"Well, *fan* does begin with the letter F. But, let's look closely now, is our fan red, white, and blue?" Ms. Bernstein asks.

"No, only white," Lena responds.

"That *car* over there!" Marcie volunteers, pointing to a toy car lying on top of the toy chest.

"Yes, Marcie, the car is red, white, and blue," Ms. Bernstein replies. "But it starts with a 'kuh' sound, doesn't it? What sound does F make?"

"Fuh!" the class shouts.

"I know, it's *face!*" Tammy exclaims. "The clown's face is red, white, and blue!"

"No, it's *pink,* white, and blue," Mac points out.

"It's the *flag!*" yells Billy. "Our flag is red, white, and blue."

"Very good, Billy," Ms. Bernstein says. "Now it's *your* turn to have us guess something. Oh, welcome back, Jon. We're in the middle of a game of Riddly Riddly Ree. Why don't you join us?"

"Riddly riddly ree," chants Billy. "I see something you don't see. It has the color black. It begins with the letter L."

"The black *letters* on Josh's shirt?" Grant offers.

"Nope."

"The *little* black chair?" Tiffany asks.

"Nope."

"The black *lines* at the top of the bulletin board," Anamaria suggests.

"Nope."

"The black *lines* painted on the chalkboard where we practice our printing!" shouts Jane.

"Nope."

"How 'bout the black *Legos*—the ones someone tried to paint black with magic markers?" Mitch asks.

"No!" giggles Billy.

"We give up, Billy," Ms. Bernstein concedes. "What's black and begins with the letter L?"

"The *'lectric* cord on the end of the fan!" he answers smugly.

Ms. Bernstein smiles. "Ah, I see. You know, a lot of children pronounce the word that way. But actually, the word is 'electric,' like this." She writes the word in uppercase letters on the chalkboard. "See, it actually begins with the letter E. OK, we didn't have a winner that time. Grant, why don't you think of the next word for us to guess?"

Ms. Bernstein eventually brings the Riddly Riddly Ree session to a close. "Boy, we had some really tricky ones today, didn't we? But fortunately, you are all really good guessers. It's always fun to think about the letters that different words start with, don't you agree?"

The children yell "Yes!" in unison.

"Today we will be making valentines for special people in our lives," Ms. Bernstein continues. The children clap and giggle with excitement as their teacher writes "VALENTINE" on the chalkboard. "What letter does the word *valentine* begin with?"

"V!" many of the children call out.

"Right! Let's have two volunteers to make a V for us on the floor." Several hands shoot into the air. "OK, Kelsie and Devin, come on up here and show us what the letter V looks like." Kelsie and Devin obligingly lie side by side on the floor next to where Ms. Bernstein is standing. The other children cluster around to watch.

Ms. Bernstein looks at Kelsie and Devin in mock puzzlement, saying, "Hmmm, something's not right here, class. This doesn't look like a V, it looks more like two sticks beside each other." Kelsie and Devin giggle.

"They should put their feet together," Julia suggests.

"Ah, good idea," Ms. Bernstein replies, as she stoops down to nudge Kelsie's and Devin's bodies into a V-like shape. "What do you think now, class? Do we have a V?"

"Yes!" the children answer.

"Good. But you know, we're going to be making a lot of valentines this morning, so one V isn't going to be enough. Each of you find a partner to make a V with on the floor." The children pair off and find empty spots around the classroom. Ms. Bernstein circulates to inspect the V's each pair has made, occasionally teasing children who have made crooked ones.

"Well done, boys and girls," Ms. Bernstein commends her students. "Now let's all come back to the circle to talk about how we might want to make our valentine cards."

The children walk quickly back to the red painted circle at the front of the room. Once everyone is seated and looking attentively in her direction, Ms. Bernstein begins: "Let's think about the people we might want to make our valentines for. Hmmm . . . we could make one for our mother or our father. We could make one for a grandparent or an aunt or uncle. We could make one for a brother or sister. We could even make one for a friend or neighbor. But I'm curious . . . why do we make valentine cards anyway?"

"To show people that we love them," Wesley answers.

"To give them something pretty," says Kyong.

"To make them feel good," says Marnie.

"Yes," Ms. Bernstein replies, "a valentine can mean all of those things. Now I realize that you all may have lots of special people in your lives, so if you finish your first valentine early you can make another one. Somewhere on your valentine, I would like you to write a special note saying how much you care about the person you're going to give it to. When you write your note, try sounding out the words on your own. Write your message on a piece of scrap paper first, then I'll help you with your spelling. Remember, the word *valentine* is written on the board in case you want to use it in your message."

Noticing that Joshua is staring out the window, Ms. Bernstein gently puts her hand on his shoulder to regain his attention but addresses her comments to the entire class. "There isn't any right or wrong way to make a valentine. I brought in some examples of valentines that other students have made. Notice how different they all are. You can make your valentine any way you like. Now please listen closely to my instructions before you return to your seats. You should all walk *quietly* to your tote trays to get your pencils, crayons, scissors, and glue. Then walk *quietly* to your seats and begin to work. You'll find red, pink, and white construction paper on every table. OK?" Ms. Bernstein pauses to be sure that all eyes are on her. "Then let's make valentines!"

The children chatter happily among themselves as they work on their valentines, but Ms. Bernstein doesn't seem to mind the noise. Instead she walks around the room, helping the children with their written messages. She is not surprised to find many misspellings in what the children have written. For example, in large black letters, Sally has written, "I LUV U MOME. WLL U BE MI VALENTINE."

Underneath Sally's words, Ms. Bernstein prints in smaller letters, "I LOVE YOU, MOMMY. WILL YOU BE MY VALENTINE?"

"This is how the words are spelled in the printed world, like in our storybooks," Ms. Bernstein tells Sally. Then, continuing to circulate about the classroom, she shows the other children how each of their messages is spelled "in the printed world."

A half-hour later, Ms. Bernstein rings a bell on her desk, and the children scramble to tidy up their tables. Several of them get a bit rowdy as they throw their discarded construction paper pieces into the recycle bins. Ms. Bernstein flicks the overhead light switch off and on, and the room immediately becomes quiet. The children whisper to each other as they finish their cleanup and then head over to the red circle.

Ms. Bernstein smiles at her class. "I like how you used your 'indoor voices' to finish cleaning up your mess. My, aren't your tables spotless!"

Questions for "Letters"

1. *Ms. Bernstein says, "Riddly riddly ree, I see something you don't see. It has the colors red, white, and blue. It begins with the letter F. What is it?" Lena's answer is "fan," referring to a fan that is only white. How might you explain her error using the idea that working memory has a limited capacity?*
2. *Why might Billy believe that the word **electric** begins with the letter L?*
3. *How does Ms. Bernstein respond to Billy's erroneous belief that **electric** begins with the letter L?*
4. *Three of the following behaviors would reflect the typical development of attention in 5- and 6-year-old children. Which one of the following behaviors, if observed in Ms. Bernstein's class, would be **least** typical?*
    a. Two children work together to form a letter V on the floor.
    b. A child looks out the window during instructions for an art project.
    c. A child works for almost 2 hours to make valentine cards for her family.
    d. A child listens for his name during the morning attendance song routine.
5. *What strategies does Ms. Bernstein use to keep her children's attention during various activities?*
6. *In which of the following instances is Ms. Bernstein using **cueing** as a classroom management strategy?*
    a. When she puts her hand on Joshua's shoulder
    *b. When she corrects Billy's spelling of **electric***
    c. When she reads a storybook to begin the school day
    d. When she tells her students about the day's art project
7. *What classroom management strategies does Ms. Bernstein use to keep her students on-task throughout the morning?*
8. *In what ways does Ms. Bernstein take diversity in children's backgrounds into account?*

CASE 30
The Star Chart

Mr. Collins doesn't use basal readers or workbooks to teach reading to his second graders. Instead, he expects his students to read at least one book a week and write a description of what they've read. Students may choose their books from a wide assortment on the bookshelves at the back of the room. Each book is color-coded to indicate how easy or difficult it is; for example, books with yellow dots are very easy, and books with red dots are quite challenging.

Once the children have completed their reading requirements each week, they stick a gold star beside their name on the star chart at the front of the room. The child with the most stars at the end of the month will, for an entire week, have the first spot in line whenever the class goes somewhere; that child will also read his or her favorite book to the class.

On the last day of September, Mr. Collins announces the first "reading winner" of the school year: Courtney has earned 17 gold stars, more than anyone else. The following morning, Mr. Collins asks Courtney to sit at the front of the room to read her favorite book. She has chosen Margret and H. A. Rey's *Curious George Goes Camping,* which is now lying open on her lap.

Courtney's voice begins to tremble as she stutters, "Je-Je-George and his f-f-friend . . . " She suddenly stops reading and looks to her teacher for assistance.

"You're doing fine, Courtney," Mr. Collins tells her. "Just slow down and have fun being the center of attention."

Courtney nods obligingly. "Je-Je-Je-George an-an-and his . . . I just can't do this, Mr. Collins."

"All right, Courtney, take a deep breath and relax. You've read this book at least a dozen times."

"I guess I don't like being the center of attention," she replies. "I don't think I can read this book in front of the class."

Mr. Collins kneels down to Courtney's level. "Does it scare you to read in front of the other kids?" he asks softly.

"Only when I'm reading up here in front of everyone," she whispers.

"You're such a lovely reader, but for some reason you're stuttering today. I wonder why."

She looks down ashamedly as she replies, "I'm afraid of messing up."

Continuing to look at Courtney, Mr. Collins stands up, then speaks loudly so the class can hear what he has to say. "Maybe it will help you to know that you're among friends. Every one of us messes up from time to time. After all, we're only human." Courtney looks at the other children, who seem to be nodding their heads in agreement.

"Reading should be fun, not scary," Mr. Collins continues. "Let's first have you tell the class why this is your favorite book and what it's about, then the two of us can read your book together."

Courtney takes a deep breath and says, "Well . . . I love Curious George because he's fun and sweet, kind of like my baby brother. In this story, Curious George goes camping . . . "

Questions for "The Star Chart"

1. *Is Mr. Collins's star chart a good idea? Why or why not?*
2. *Mr. Collins is trying to motivate his students to read by giving them gold stars for each book that they've read and then awarding special privileges to the student who reads the greatest number of books each month. For which children is this approach likely to be motivating?*
3. *For which children is Mr. Collins's approach **not** likely to be motivating?*
4. *Is the star chart likely to promote the development of self-regulation? Why or why not?*
5. *Is Mr. Collins wise to let his students make their own choices about what they read?*
6. *Is Courtney experiencing state anxiety or trait anxiety? Is it facilitating anxiety or debilitating anxiety?*
7. *How would a **behaviorist** be most likely to explain Courtney's anxiety while reading in front of the class?*
    a. *Courtney may have seen other students make mistakes while reading and be ridiculed by their peers.*
    b. *Courtney was probably born with an anxious temperament, and so she is easily rattled by unexpected events.*
    c. *At some point in Courtney's past, a bad experience caused her to associate reading with unpleasant circumstances.*
    d. *Courtney attributes her success on the star chart to luck, and she doubts whether she will be so lucky when reading to her peers.*
8. *How would a **social cognitive theorist** be most likely to explain Courtney's anxiety while reading in front of the class?*
    a. *Courtney may have seen other students make mistakes while reading and be ridiculed by their peers.*
    b. *Courtney was probably born with an anxious temperament, and so she is easily rattled by unexpected events.*
    c. *At some point in Courtney's past, a bad experience caused her to associate reading with unpleasant circumstances.*
    d. *Courtney attributes her success on the star chart to luck, and she doubts whether she will be so lucky when reading to her peers.*
9. *What additional strategies might Mr. Collins employ to address Courtney's anxiety?*

CASE 31
The Bulletin Board

As his third graders work in pairs to proofread one another's short stories, Mr. Wilson begins to tack some of his students' spelling, mathematics, and social studies papers on the "Look What I Did" bulletin board. As he thumbs through the stack of papers in front of him, he notices a frown on Jordan's face. "What's the matter, Jordan?" he asks.

"My sister says I won't get any stickers next year 'cause I'll be in fourth grade. She says I'll be too old for stickers then. Is that true, Mr. Wilson?"

Kneeling down beside Jordan, Mr. Wilson replies, "Well, that probably depends on who your teacher is. I know some fourth-grade teachers who give stickers, and I know others who don't. Why do you ask?"

"Well, I'm in the third grade already, and I've *never* gotten a sticker on one of my papers, so I never get anything put up on the bulletin board. I was sorta hoping I might get one some day so I could have my paper hung up."

"I've never had a paper hung up, either, Mr. Wilson," Emma points out.

"Me, neither," adds Xias. "No matter how hard I try, I'm just not good enough for the bulletin board."

Mr. Wilson is dumbfounded. He's never realized that he has consistently excluded some children from his exhibits. "But, hey," he responds aloud, "it's only February. We still have lots of time for improving our study habits." He notices that the entire class is listening to the conversation.

Jordan looks frustrated. "I always make mistakes on my stuff even though I don't mean to. Look," he says as he points to the papers on the bulletin board, "all of these have stickers. All of them! And do you notice something else? They all have A's on them!"

"Yeah," Xias agrees. "See? Tonya, A in math. Edwin, A in reading. Olga, A in math. Brad, A in history. Tori, A+ in science."

Mr. Wilson looks more closely at the papers he's posted. "You know what? You children are right. I was discriminating against some of you, and I didn't even know it. I think we'd better fix this situation right away."

"All right!" shouts Jordan. "So how are we gonna fix it?"

"Well, this bulletin board belongs to you—my students—not to me. How about if everybody brings me what you think is your best work—one paper for each of you—and we'll display it? And if you don't want to participate, that's OK too." Mr. Wilson notices many of his students eagerly rummaging through their desks in search of things they might want to show off.

"Can we change what's up there once a week?" Emma asks.

"That's a great idea, Emma. Starting today, *you* choose what you want to go on *your* bulletin board. Hmmm . . . I guess I'd better take down the things that are up here now and pass them back to their owners."

As he does so, Mr. Wilson tells himself, "And from now on, any child who shows improvement receives a sticker and a note saying 'Good progress!'"

Questions for "The Bulletin Board"

1. *What might be Mr. Wilson's rationale for posting good papers on the bulletin board?*
2. *The concept of **self-efficacy** refers to a learner's belief about his or her ability to perform a certain task successfully. How might the original bulletin board (i.e., the one that displays only the A papers) affect the self-efficacy of Mr. Wilson's students?*
3. *What problems do you see in Mr. Wilson's practice of posting good papers on the bulletin board?*
4. *Xias says, "No matter how hard I try, I'm just not good enough for the bulletin board." From this statement, you might reasonably suspect that which one of the following is true about Xias?*
    a. He has facilitating anxiety.
    b. He has learned helplessness.
    c. He is manifesting a self-fulfilling prophecy.
    d. He is exhibiting a phenomenon commonly known as the "personal fable."
5. *What kind of attribution is Xias making when he says, "No matter how hard I try, I'm just not good enough for the bulletin board"? How is such an attribution likely to affect his future performance?*
6. *Describe two different strategies Mr. Wilson might use to help Xias form more productive attributions for his performance.*
7. *To what does Mr. Wilson attribute some students' consistently poor performance? Is his attribution an accurate one?*
8. *Is it appropriate for Mr. Wilson to give stickers when his students show progress, even if their performance is only marginally satisfactory?*
9. *By showcasing students' best work on a bulletin board, Mr. Wilson is probably promoting performance goals. Describe two different strategies Mr. Wilson might use to encourage students to develop mastery goals instead.*

CASE 32
Halloween

As her third graders head out the door at the end of one school day late in October, Ms. Gonzales hands each of them a letter to take home to their parents or guardians:

> Dear Friends,
>
> This coming Friday, we will celebrate Halloween with our traditional costume parade and class party. If your child does not have a costume but would like to participate in the parade, the school has a number of costumes available. Please call the school secretary, Mrs. Witherspoon, if you think your child might like to borrow one.
>
> Our room mothers have been busily baking cupcakes and purchasing other party treats. We would certainly welcome additional contributions from those of you who have the time and energy to provide them. Because a few students in our class have either food allergies or diabetes, I would ask that you not send any items that include either *sugar* or *peanuts*. I suggest fruit, sugarless gum, or inexpensive plastic trinkets as items that the children might enjoy.
>
> If you would like to help out at our party, I would certainly love to have you join us. The Halloween celebration here at Northrup Elementary is always fun for parents as well as children. Feel free to give me a call if you have any questions.
>
> Sincerely,
Ms. Celeste Gonzales

On Friday morning, most of Ms. Gonzales's students arrive with their costumes in their backpacks or in grocery bags. Although they are clearly excited about the afternoon's Halloween festivities, Ms. Gonzales tells them that it will be "business as usual" in her classroom until after lunch. After taking attendance and collecting lunch money, Ms. Gonzales calls one of her reading groups to the reading table and instructs the other children to continue working on the math problems they began the day before.

Ms. Gonzales notices that her students seem considerably more hyperactive and distractible than usual this morning. The children in her reading group don't seem to be focusing on the story they are reading. Instead, they keep looking at the clock on the wall or exchanging meaningful glances. A stern look from their teacher is usually enough to get them back on-task, but rarely for very long.

Meanwhile, Ms. Gonzales is also keeping an eye on the other children in her classroom—those who are supposed to be working independently on their math assignment. Everyone is quite fidgety today, and there is a great deal of whispering from one desk to another. Ms. Gonzales finds herself having to call out several children's names as a way of silencing them.

During recess, she looks over her students' math papers. The papers are messier than usual, and about half of the children didn't complete all the assigned problems. "I hope that recess will help them release some of their energy," she thinks. "Otherwise it's going to be a *very* long morning."

After recess, Ms. Gonzales gives the weekly spelling test. All of the words this week are related to Halloween.

"OK, class, now that you have your paper and pencils ready, let's begin. The first word is *Halloween*. Today we are having a Halloween party. *Halloween*." The children giggle, then write the word on their papers.

"Next word. *Pumpkin*. Today our class will carve a pumpkin during our party. *Pumpkin*."

"Are we really carving a pumpkin?" asks Tandy.

"Yes," Ms. Gonzales replies. The children clap and squirm in their seats.

"Word number three. *Party*. We will have a party only if you all calm down. *Party*." She smiles as the children try to sit more quietly in their seats.

Note: In later years, Ms. Gonzales planned group projects for days on which afternoon class parties were scheduled. Such projects allowed the children to talk with one another without getting off-task.

Questions for "Halloween"

1. What are potential strengths and weaknesses of the letter that Ms. Gonzales sends home to parents and guardians? In your analysis, draw on principles of effective parent–teacher communication.
2. Ms. Gonzales gives some children a stern look to get them back on-task. Her strategy can best be described as an example of which one of the following?
    a. Cueing
    b. Operant conditioning
    c. Vicarious punishment
    d. Negative reinforcement
3. What classroom management strategies does Ms. Gonzales implement prior to the Halloween celebration?
4. Should teachers try to teach academics on the day of a class party?
5. Is it a good idea for Ms. Gonzales to focus the week's spelling list on words related to Halloween?

6.   *Some parents prefer that their children not celebrate Halloween, often for religious reasons. Is it appropriate to ask such parents to keep their children home on Halloween? Why or why not?*

7.   *What would you do with the math assignments that were handed in on the day of the party? Would you grade them as usual, even though some of the children did not complete them?*

CASE 33
Culture Shock

Mr. Beezley has been an elementary school teacher for many years, but teaching school in a small agricultural town in northwestern New Mexico is a new experience for him. Although he's been in town since early July, he hasn't attended any of the social events—the chili suppers, the donkey basketball games, the fall festival organized by the high school students—in the local community. By September, he's acquired a reputation as a cold and arrogant Easterner.

Little does the community realize that Mr. Beezley is feeling quite overwhelmed in his new teaching position. Most of his students are Navajo children with very different backgrounds from those of his former students back in Massachusetts. He spends his evenings and weekends reading everything he can about Navajo culture, and he spends hours upon hours developing lessons and activities to meet the academic needs of his new students.

The classroom behaviors of Mr. Beezley's students present an additional challenge. Many of the children seem to have trouble staying in their seats and working independently. On one occasion early in the school year, Mr. Beezley is quite surprised to see a boy in his class get out of his seat to help a classmate with a geography assignment. He approaches the two students to see if they need help, but they continue to talk to each other as if he weren't even there. He is shocked by their bold behavior. Back in Massachusetts, his presence alone would have been enough to silence any misbehaving students. At a loss for how to respond, he decides to do nothing for the time being.

A few minutes later, two other boys leave their seats to work with classmates. Having had enough of such behavior, Mr. Beezley reprimands them for getting up without permission. The boys are visibly shocked by his reaction, yet Mr. Beezley has never seen children so blatantly disrespectful. He angrily snatches the assignments on which the two students have been collaborating and insists that they return to their seats.

A few children are obviously quite upset by their teacher's demeanor, and so other children go to comfort them. Mr. Beezley can't believe that anyone has the nerve to get up after all that has happened. The continuing misbehavior of his students utterly astonishes him.

"In my classroom, I expect you all to do your own work," he tells his class firmly. "Why are you all so insistent on doing everyone *else's* work?"

"We always help one another . . . ," Maria responds.

" . . . because it's the right thing to do," John continues, completing Maria's thought.

"How can we learn anything . . . ," says Anna.

" . . . if one of us doesn't understand?" adds Victor.

"Good grief," Mr. Beezley thinks to himself, "these children answer questions as a collective group. They can't even *talk* as individuals!" He is so taken aback by the fact that his students are rudely interrupting one another that he doesn't even hear what they're telling him.

Determined to nip the children's "inappropriate" behaviors in the bud, Mr. Beezley goes to the main office after school to seek the advice of the school principal. Waiting patiently while the principal finishes a telephone conversation, he suddenly finds several of his students standing in front of him with their parents.

"Come . . . ," says one of the parents.

" . . . and join us for dinner . . . ," adds another.

" . . . for it will give us a chance . . . ," continues a third.

" . . . to get to know one other," finishes a fourth.

Mr. Beezley is totally confused. Does everyone live in the same house? Or, alternatively, is he supposed to go to four different homes for dinner in a single evening?

That evening, after following the parents' directions to the nearby Navajo Nation, Mr. Beezley finds himself at the home of one of his students. As he approaches the front door, he hears a great deal of laughter coming from the house. He expects to find a party inside but discovers that it is merely a gathering of several of his students' families sitting around a large table. The children's parents are telling tales from their own childhood, and one often interrupts another to insert additional anecdotes. They invite Mr. Beezley to sit down, and for the next 2 hours they enthrall him with their colorful conversation. He discovers many aspects of Navajo culture that he had been completely unaware of—for example, how different families often live very intermingled lives.

After dinner, when a neighbor's truck breaks down, the entire group goes to the man's aid. Two parents drive to town for needed parts, and upon their return parents and children alike assist in the engine's repair. Several people hold lights, others work under the hood, and still others offer occasional suggestions and strategies.

By this time, Mr. Beezley feels comfortable enough that he is laughing and joking with the others. But he realizes that he still has a great deal to learn about the local Navajo culture. He suspects that in the days to come he'll learn as much from his new students as they are likely to learn from him.

Note: Mr. Beezley spent many hours at the Navajo Nation after that, and he was always greeted affectionately when he arrived. He was frequently invited to join the Nation's sacred rituals, and he eventually became an honorary member of the community.

Questions for "Culture Shock"

1. *In Navajo culture, an older child may often assist a younger child with a new task. The benefits of such assistance are most easily explained using _____ view of cognitive development.*
   a. *Piaget's*
   b. *Vygotsky's*
   c. *behaviorists'*
   d. *information processing theorists'*
2. *Should Mr. Beezley change his expectations for students' classroom behavior in his new teaching situation? Why or why not?*
3. *In general, to what extent is it appropriate for teachers to adjust their expectations and teaching practices to the cultural backgrounds of their students?*
4. *Describe at least two different strategies Mr. Beezley might use that would be compatible with the children's cultural background.*
5. *Identify at least two different ways in which Mr. Beezley might assess his students' learning in a manner consistent with their culture.*
6. *Might there be occasions in which Mr. Beezley should insist that his students work independently?*
7. *If you were Mr. Beezley, how might you structure classroom tasks so that students acquire the ability to work independently as well as cooperatively?*
8. *Mr. Beezley has difficulty making sense of the dinner invitation from his students' parents. Explain his difficulty using the concept of knowledge construction.*
9. *Beginning teachers are often so busy preparing their daily lessons and familiarizing themselves with school procedures that they lose sight of the larger community within which they work. As a new teacher, how might you get to know something about the culture or cultures in which your students have been raised?*

CASE 34
Getting a Drink

Dari feels uncomfortable as she makes the seemingly endless trip from her desk to the drinking fountain at the back of the room. If she had a choice, she wouldn't make the trip at all. She is well aware that her classmates resent her being allowed to get a drink whenever she wants to, whereas they have to wait until recess or lunch. They know that the medicine she takes every morning makes her thirsty, but they still tease her about being "Teacher's Pet."

"Why can't the others get drinks when they want to?" she wonders. "It wouldn't be any big deal. Besides, Ms. Patterson is *always* drinking her coffee. She carries that stupid coffee mug around so much that it looks as if it's attached to her body."

"Hey, Ms. Patterson, can I get a drink?" Craig calls out. "It's a really hot day, and I'm thirsty."

"Of course not, Craig. You know my rule about that." Ms. Patterson is obviously annoyed at his question.

Craig persists. "It's not fair. *You* can drink your coffee whenever you want to."

"I never said life is fair," Ms. Patterson replies. "I'm the teacher, so I have certain privileges. I need to have something to drink because I do most of the talking and my mouth gets dry. Besides, my job is to make sure that you children learn, and I can't do that if you're running to the drinking fountain all the time. It won't kill you to wait until recess to get a drink."

"But we could use a water bottle," Huong suggests.

"No, that won't work. A couple of years ago, I let my students bring water bottles to school, and they used them to squirt one another all the time. When are you people going to learn that *no* means *no?*"

"But you let Dari go to the fountain whenever she wants to," Shelby points out.

"Dari has medical problems," Ms. Patterson responds. "Anyway, I know that she'll only get a drink if she really, really needs one. Right, Dari?"

Dari nods self-consciously and then tries to make herself smaller by scrunching low in her seat.

"Yeah, she's special, all right," Guy scoffs. "She's Teacher's Pet."

Note: This was Ms. Patterson's last year in the classroom.

Questions for "Getting a Drink"

1. *Ms. Patterson lets Dari use the water fountain because of her special medical needs, knowing that Dari will not abuse the privilege. Dari feels uncomfortable about the situation because, as she is well aware, her classmates resent her preferential treatment. If she had a choice, Dari wouldn't use the water fountain at*

all. *The privilege of using the water fountain during class is, for Dari, most consistent with which one of the following behaviorist concepts?*

    a. *Extinction*

    b. *Punishment*

    c. *Negative reinforcement*

    d. *Secondary reinforcement*

2.   *What basic student needs may not be being met in Ms. Patterson's classroom?*

3.   *Some motivation theorists propose that two conditions are essential for* **intrinsic motivation:** *a sense of competence (i.e., self-efficacy) and a sense of self-determination (i.e., a belief that one has some control over the course of one's own life). With these conditions in mind, decide whether Ms. Patterson is promoting intrinsic motivation to behave appropriately in her classroom.*

4.   *Is Ms. Patterson's decision not to allow students to get a drink during class a reasonable one? Why or why not?*

5.   *Ms. Patterson continually drinks coffee in front of her students. Should teachers be allowed to enjoy classroom rights forbidden to students? Why or why not?*

6.   *Many psychologists believe that human beings have a basic need for* **relatedness**—*a need to feel socially connected to others and have others' love and respect. Students with special medical conditions may, like Dari, sometimes have difficulty making friends at school. What strategies might a teacher use to help Dari meet her need for relatedness?*

CASE 35
Summer School

To be honest, I accepted a summer school position at Cumberland Elementary because I thought the class would be an easy one to teach. I would have only five students and work half-days yet still get a full-time salary. But I was sadly mistaken in my belief that the position would be an effortless one. For one thing, teaching five students with special needs was far more difficult than teaching a classroom of 30 nondisabled students. In addition, I discovered that there is probably no such thing as working only half a day when you're a teacher: After teaching my class every morning, I spent the afternoon creating individualized lessons to meet each child's specific academic needs in reading, writing, and mathematics. By the end of the first week, it was clear that my "part-time" job would consume my entire summer.

I don't think I could have had five more different students if I had tried. Ben, who was 9, suffered from a progressive neurological condition that had left him blind and was slowly eroding his mental capabilities. Although usually a kind and gentle child, he would have unpredictable outbursts that disrupted whatever the rest of us might be doing. For example, several times a day he would suddenly scream and start punching the air with his fists until he eventually found something solid—a desk, a wall, or perhaps another student. He would then continue punching that object or person until I physically restrained him. I didn't feel that I could reprimand Ben for such outbursts, as they were undoubtedly a symptom of his neurological impairment.

Eleven-year-old Hannah had been sexually molested by her mother's boyfriend on numerous occasions over the past 2 years, and she now displayed a variety of bizarre behaviors. For example, she would frequently reach out to touch or grab other students in inappropriate places. On several occasions, always when I was preoccupied with Ben, she would take off her clothes and rub her body against different objects around the room—her desk, her art box, pencils, you name it. When she was nervous about something, she would compulsively rock back and forth in her chair, or she would pull at her hair until she left a bald spot.

Meanwhile, 9-year-old Cameron had a distinctly sadistic streak. He would hit his classmates, often on the nose or in the eyes, then smile as they screamed out in pain. He spit on people just to see how they'd react. If they expressed disgust, he'd spit on them again. If they lashed out in anger, he'd hit them and run away.

My other two students had been diagnosed as having mental retardation. One of them, Arnold, was a sweet-tempered 8-year-old who had Down syndrome. The other, 12-year-old Steven, had no genetic disorders but had been officially labeled as having mental retardation based on his low scores on a series of intelligence tests. Steven's prior schooling had been limited to just part of one year in a first-grade classroom in inner-city Chicago. His mother had pulled him out after a bullet grazed his leg while he was walking to school one morning; fearing for her son's safety, she would not let him outside the apartment after that, not even to play, and certainly not to walk the six blocks to school. When a truant officer finally appeared at the door one evening in May five years later, Steven and his mother quickly packed their bags and moved to the small Colorado town in which I was teaching. They found residence with Steven's aunt, who persuaded Steven to go back to school. After considering Steven's intelligence and achievement test scores, the school psychologist recommended that he attend my summer school class.

Perhaps my biggest challenge that summer was to keep my five students from physically harming one another. Numerous disputes occurred every day, often when I least expected them. For example, we might be in the middle of a lesson when, all of a sudden, one child or another would start yelling and screaming in a classic temper tantrum.

One day especially stands out in my mind. We had been studying nutrition, and so I had asked each of the children to bring in some fresh vegetables to make a large salad for our morning snack. Steven arrived with a can of green beans.

"What the hell is that?" Cameron yelled from across the room. Cameron cursed frequently. Initially I had thought that he did it to gain attention, but I soon learned that cursing was the standard manner of speaking in his family. I usually ignored his foul language, reasoning that I had more important behaviors of his to address.

"It's green beans!" Steven stated proudly.

"What's going on?" asked Ben, who could not see what Steven had brought.

Hannah answered his question. "Steven brought a *can* of green beans."

"If they're in a can, then they're not fresh," Ben pointed out.

"The hell they ain't!" was Steven's angry reply. "Me and Momma got them off the shelf this morning!"

Oh my, I thought, what do I do now? And then it suddenly hit me: Steven quite possibly wasn't mentally retarded at all! It was his prior knowledge—or rather, his *lack* of it—that was interfering with his academic progress. After all, he didn't even know what a "fresh" vegetable was. My mind was reeling, and mentally I was quickly revising my objectives for Steven. He needed to learn the basics—not only in reading, writing, and math but also with regard to the many facts and concepts that most children his age had already acquired.

While I was pondering Steven's situation, Cameron darted across the classroom and whacked Steven's nose. "Stupid kid!" he yelled. "You don't even know what's fresh!"

Despite my best efforts to restrain Cameron, he continued to attack Steven all morning long. When Steven's mother arrived at noon to pick up her son, I shared the day's unfortunate events with her. Remembering why she had taken her son out of first grade in Chicago, I fully expected her to remove him from my classroom as well. Instead she told me, "Ms. Teacher, I think it's time we did something about this aggression. Recess ain't cuttin' it for these kids. They're all still too full of piss and vinegar to study."

"No kidding," I silently agreed while tightly holding Cameron's hands to keep him from inflicting further damage on Steven. The bus driver was standing in the doorway wondering why the four children he usually took home—Cameron, Hannah, Ben, and Arnold—weren't ready to leave. The driver's assistant picked up Cameron and carried him onto the bus. Hannah left the building flapping her arms. Ben was holding Arnold's left elbow and walking toward the bus when he suddenly grabbed Arnold's hair and gave it a quick yank.

"No pulling hair, Ben!" yelled Arnold. Ben momentarily fingered the strands of hair he had pulled from Arnold's scalp. The strands drifted to the ground, and Arnold continued to guide Ben toward the bus as if nothing had happened.

Maybe Steven's mother was right—maybe my students needed an outlet for all their pent-up energy, because recess simply wasn't "cuttin' it." I wondered if vigorous physical activity first thing in the morning might relieve some of their energy. We tried everything, it seemed—kickball, basketball, tag, running races—yet I saw little improvement in their behavior when we finally settled down for academic work later in the morning. Then one day I found plastic hockey sticks and a hollow plastic puck in the back of the gymnasium closet. I wasn't sure that I could trust my students with such potentially dangerous equipment, yet I decided to take a chance and teach them the basics of field hockey, albeit an indoor version of the game.

I knew that I needed to adapt the game for Ben, who was blind. So I had players on the "blue team" wear high-pitched Christmas sleigh bells tied around their wrists; "red team" players wore similar bells tied to their shoe laces. I sliced open the handles of the hockey sticks and inserted lower-pitched bells, then glued the handles shut again, so that Ben would be able to tell where each player's hockey stick was on the playing field. I put a loud buzzer inside the plastic puck. I attached electronic beepers to the tops and sides of the goals.

We went to the gym first thing each morning for a half-hour of hockey. All five students really got into the game, and not one of them ever tried to hit a classmate with a hockey stick. Except for Ben, whose neurological condition seemed to worsen as the summer wore on, the aggressive behavior in my classroom completely stopped once we began our daily hockey games. I honestly don't know why. Maybe hockey provided more of an outlet for their energy than our other activities had. Maybe the game forced them to depend on one another in ways they had never had to before. Maybe my allowing them to play with potentially dangerous equipment communicated a sense of trust that they didn't want to abuse. Maybe their change in behavior was just a fluke and had nothing to do with the hockey games at all.

Oddly, it was Cameron who taught me how to predict Ben's temper tantrums. One day he said to me, "Teacher, I don't think Ben should be playing hockey right now."

"Why not, Cameron?"

"He's getting ready to be mean."

"How do you know that?"

"Look at his ears. They get red whenever he's ready to hurt someone." I looked at Ben's ears and saw that Cameron had described them accurately. I guided Ben over to the punching bag, where he proceeded to have a violent temper tantrum, taking out much of his anger on the bag. The other four children continued their hockey game as if nothing out of the ordinary were happening.

With my students' energy expended in the gym first thing every morning, they were better able to focus on academic tasks. Steven improved by leaps and bounds that summer; he was like a sponge that absorbed as much as he possibly could. The others made a little progress on their reading, writing, and mathematics, although probably not enough to brag about. On the other hand, all five of my students made dramatic gains in their social skills. By the end of the summer, each of them was able to express anger in an appropriate verbal fashion instead of striking out physically.

> *Note:* By the time Steven reached high school, he was enrolling in regular classes and maintaining a 3.5 average; the last time I spoke with his mother, she told me that he was planning to attend college the following September. Meanwhile, Hannah and Arnold remained in self-contained classrooms for several years to follow. Ben died a year after he left my classroom from complications due to his condition. I have no idea what happened to Cameron.

Questions for "Summer School"

1. *At the beginning of the summer, which student most clearly shows a deficit in perspective-taking ability?*
    a. *Arnold*
    b. *Ben*
    c. *Cameron*
    d. *Hannah*
2. *Arnold has Down syndrome. Three of the following instructional strategies are appropriate for children with this condition. Which one is **least** likely to be appropriate?*
    a. *Explain assigned tasks in specific, concrete terms.*
    b. *Assign the same academic tasks that you give nondisabled classmates.*
    c. *Present new material more slowly than you would for other students.*
    d. *Provide considerable scaffolding to facilitate successful performance.*
3. *When Cameron curses ("What the hell is that?"), his teacher ignores him. Is this an appropriate reaction to Cameron's inappropriate behavior?*
4. *At one point, the teacher concludes that Steven doesn't have mental retardation. Is her conclusion an accurate one?*
5. *What benefits might the daily hockey games have?*

CASE 36
Math Baseball

The students in Mr. Balcom's sixth-grade mathematics class have counted off by twos as a way of dividing themselves into two teams for a game of math baseball. The "Red Sox" have gone to the right side of the room, and the "White Sox" have gone to the left side. Each team is now lined up behind a strip of masking tape on the floor.

The students watch as Mr. Balcom draws miniature baseball diamonds on both ends of the chalkboard and attaches a small, magnetic picture of a baseball player at each "home plate." He then writes the same math problem just below the two diamonds he's drawn. As he places his piece of chalk in the chalk tray, he shouts, "Go!"

The two students at the front of each line—Tyrell and Corey—race to the board. Tyrell, who is playing for the Red Sox, solves the problem first. Because he's earned a "hit" for his team, he moves his team's baseball player to "first base." Corey is still struggling with the problem, but he knows that Mr. Balcom won't let him leave the board until he solves it correctly.

"I can't believe you haven't figured it out yet, Corey," Mr. Balcom admonishes him. "Come on, you can do this. Here, look at the way Tyrell did it. . . . Never mind, don't get so upset. It's only the first out for your team. There's still plenty of time to make runs."

Corey hears his White Sox teammates moan. He marks an out for his team on the board and then walks slowly to the end of his line. A couple of his teammates pat him on the back as he walks by, but others are less kind.

"Thanks a lot for nothing, Corey."

"I can't believe you missed such an easy problem."

"Are you stupid or something?"

As the game continues, Corey's mind is more on the clock than on the game. The minutes tick by ever so slowly. As the other team members have their turn "at bat," Corey moves closer and closer to the front of the line, and he soon finds himself standing right behind the masking tape once again.

"One more out and we lose the game," Chip whispers from behind him. "Come on, man, don't screw it up this time."

"I *hate* this game!" Corey thinks as he watches Mr. Balcom write the problem he knows he will have to solve.

"No goofing around, young man," Mr. Balcom warns as Corey approaches the board. "I expect you to show us what you know this time. Just think it through . . . "

Note: Corey was an extremely shy boy who didn't like being the center of attention. Although he had earned an A in math the preceding year, he earned an F in Mr. Balcom's class. His achievement in math slowly improved in the years that followed—a D the next year, and a C– the year after that—and he earned B's fairly consistently in high school.

Questions for "Math Baseball"

1. *Corey is most likely experiencing which one of the following?*
    a. *Hot cognition*
    b. *Stereotype threat*
    c. *Facilitating anxiety*
    d. *Debilitating anxiety*
2. *What conditions are contributing to Corey's feelings of discomfort during the math baseball game?*
3. *Mr. Balcom says several things to Corey, presumably in an attempt to motivate him. Are his statements likely to be effective in this respect?*
4. *How is Corey's experience in this class apt to affect his self-efficacy?*
5. *Is the baseball game likely to help Corey improve his math skills?*
6. *To what extent is the baseball game likely to be motivating to the other students in the class?*
7. *Why does Corey's math performance drop from A-level achievement one year to failure in Mr. Balcom's class the following year?*
8. *If you were Corey's math teacher the following year (i.e., in seventh grade), what strategies might you use to improve Corey's self-efficacy and math performance?*
9. *How might you change the baseball game so that it doesn't have such a negative impact on some students?*

CASE 37
The Stand-Up Comic

Although 13-year-old Connor arrives at Kennedy Middle School each day clean and well groomed, his threadbare clothes set him apart from the other students. After 2 months, he hasn't found a single friend—a single classmate who will accept him as he is.

Connor's impoverished circumstances are called to everyone's attention at the beginning of third-hour history class one day. When Mr. DeVenney is temporarily distracted by a message from the main office, Zach calls out, "Hey, what's with wearing the same two pairs of pants all the time? Haven't you noticed that they're way too short for you and are, like, falling apart?"

"I can't help it if my family doesn't have much money," Connor replies sullenly.

"Like, how poor *are* you? I see you eating a peanut butter sandwich and drinking Kool-Aid every day at lunch. Don't you know that they have free lunches for people like you? Maybe you'd get a little more variety." The other students are all looking in Connor's direction.

Connor is quiet for a moment, but his face suddenly lights up when he thinks of a witty comeback: "My family's so poor that we take a rolling pin to mash out a piece of bread, pour catsup on it, and call it pizza." Many of the students giggle at his joke, although a few seem to feel a bit awkward about doing so.

"Of course," he adds, "my brother puts on a newspaper hat, walks around the block a few times with the pizza in his hand, then rings our doorbell. Now we're really feeling all hotsy-totsy 'cause we're getting home delivery!" The entire class bursts into laughter, and Mr. DeVenney looks up to see what is going on.

"It's sad, though," Connor continues. "Sometimes my brother forgets where we live, and then the pizza gets cold." By this time, the class is practically rolling in the aisles. Mr. DeVenney is not quite sure what has just happened, but he's pleased to see Connor finally interacting with his peers.

"Hey, you're all right, dude," Zach calls out. Connor is grinning from ear to ear.

"OK, you two," Mr. DeVenney tells them warmly but sternly, "I think you've taken enough of our valuable time. Let's get started with today's lesson. As you should remember from yesterday, we've been talking about the Industrial Revolution . . . "

As he proceeds with his lesson plan, Mr. DeVenney has trouble keeping the class on-task, because Connor, who's always been so quiet and well behaved, interjects *I'm so poor . . .* jokes as often as he can think of them. The class responds more enthusiastically with each new joke, and Connor is obviously delighted by the attention.

"Oh well," Mr. DeVenney thinks, "what's wrong with not making any progress for one day? The kid's having his moment in the sun. It'll probably never happen again."

By the beginning of December, Mr. DeVenney has lost all control of his third-hour history class. Although Connor seems to have exhausted his supply of *I'm so poor . . .* jokes, he has developed a repertoire of jokes on virtually every other topic—school, sports, politics, religion, even the weather. Mr. DeVenney is at a loss for what to do. He has tried ignoring Connor, reprimanding him in front of his classmates, sending him to the office, keeping him after school, making him eat lunch in the teacher's lounge, sending notes home, and, on one occasion, meeting with his parents. Yet Connor's joke telling continues unabated.

Exasperated after one especially rough day, Mr. DeVenney keeps Connor after class. "No matter what I do, you won't shut up," he admonishes his class clown. "Thanks to you, we've hardly accomplished *anything* in the last few weeks."

"I'm sorry," Connor replies a little sheepishly. "But you know, Mr. D., it feels good to be liked for a change."

Mr. DeVenney suddenly understands why Connor has been behaving as he has. "I see. Hmmm . . . " He pauses, rubbing his chin as he thinks the situation through. "OK, then, I tell you what. I'll let you tell one joke at the very beginning of class each day. I'll even let you stand at the front of the room to tell it, like a stand-up comic would do. I have one condition, though: You cannot tell any jokes that degrade other human beings in any way. In other words, no religious, racial, ethnic, sexist, or sexual orientation put-downs. And remember, you can only tell *one* joke a day. What do you think?"

"How about two jokes?"

"One joke, and it has to be at the beginning of the period."

"It's a deal," Connor replies as he reaches out to shake Mr. DeVenney's hand.

After his second-hour class each day, Mr. DeVenney finds a chair at the back of the classroom so that Connor can have the "stage" to himself when he arrives at the beginning of third hour. Connor is never late to class, but he usually arrives just before the bell rings so that he can make a grand entrance. He tells his joke for the day, priding himself on his delivery and timing as much as on the joke itself. Despite his classmates' frequent encouragement for an encore, Connor keeps his word to Mr. DeVenney, limiting himself to a single joke and then taking his seat.

"This is working well," Mr. DeVenney concludes. "Once Connor finishes his joke, I seem to have my students' full attention for the rest of the period. As a matter of fact, I can't think of any other time in my teaching career when I've had a class so completely under control."

Connor continues "performing" in his third-hour history class for several weeks. Then one day he approaches Mr. DeVenney after school. "I . . . uh . . . I don't think I need to tell jokes anymore, Mr. D."

"Oh?"

"Well . . . I have friends now. I eat lunch with them and stuff. We do things together—things that don't cost money—and we hang out."

"And what does all this have to do with your jokes?"

"Well, my jokes gave me a chance to let the other kids get to know me, and I liked all the attention I was getting. But now that I have friends, I can get attention in other ways."

"That's a very insightful observation, Connor. I'm really proud of you."

"Well, thanks, Mr. D. . . . thanks for everything."

"Damn!" Mr. DeVenney says to himself as Connor walks out the door. "I'm going to miss those jokes."

Note: Connor eventually became a successful chemical engineer and provided several college scholarships to boys residing at a homeless shelter where he volunteered his time every Saturday.

Questions for "The Stand-Up Comic"

1. *Many young adolescents believe that certain kinds of clothes are desirable and other kinds are definitely **not** desirable. They are apt to try to conform to these perceptions of what's "cool" and what's not—even if adults and peers never talk about clothes. Which one of the following concepts best explains this phenomenon?*
   a. *Attachment*
   b. *Peer pressure*
   c. *Self-socialization*
   d. *Social information processing*
2. *To what extent does Mr. DeVenney display withitness at the beginning of the case study?*
3. *Connor's joke telling increases once he discovers that his jokes make his classmates laugh. This change can best be explained using which one of the following concepts?*
   a. *Induction*
   b. *Personal fable*
   c. *Operant conditioning*
   d. *Vicarious reinforcement*
4. *When Mr. DeVenney keeps Connor after class to discuss the problem behavior, what does he do to preserve Connor's self-esteem?*
5. *Is Mr. DeVenney's strategy for addressing Connor's distracting influence an effective one? Why or why not?*
6. *Would it have been better for Mr. DeVenney to let Connor tell his joke at the end of class rather than at the beginning? Why or why not?*

7. *How might Mr. DeVenney act differently in the fall to prevent the out-of-control situation he has this December?*
8. *If you discover that a student is being ostracized by his or her classmates, as Connor initially is, what might you do to help?*

CASE 38
The Perfectionist

Each time 13-year-old William begins a new drawing or painting in Mr. Mercurio's art class, he quickly becomes dissatisfied with his efforts and tosses what he has done into the wastepaper basket. After 3 months, he has yet to submit a completed project. Unless the situation changes, Mr. Mercurio realizes he may have no choice but to give the boy a failing grade.

Hoping to curtail William's perfectionistic behavior, Mr. Mercurio scolds him for wasting art materials. Although William doesn't like being reprimanded, his wasteful behavior doesn't diminish; if anything, it's becoming more frequent. At wit's end, Mr. Mercurio finally keeps William after class one day to discuss the situation.

"Why does your work have to be perfect, William?"

"Because I don't want it to look stupid."

"I don't know of *any* artwork that is 'stupid,' William, and I certainly don't know of any that is perfect. In my class, the most important things are to do your best and to work at improving your skills as the year progresses."

"But my best is never good enough. I'm not good at art. I don't want the other kids to see how bad I really am."

"I see. Well, then, why don't we try a different approach? Let's see if we can find today's project in the wastepaper basket . . . Ah, yes, here it is. How about finishing it at home tonight? You can bring it to me first thing tomorrow morning. That way, only you and I will see what you have done."

William reluctantly agrees and takes the crumpled paper that Mr. Mercurio is handing him.

At lunch time the following day, Mr. Mercurio finds William eating alone in the cafeteria and sits down beside him. "William, I waited for you this morning, but you didn't show up."

"I didn't have time to see you."

"Did you bring your art project?"

"No. I couldn't finish it because I had to do my chores."

"Do you think you will ever finish it?"

William hesitates. "Probably not."

"Why?"

"Because it looks ridiculous. Let's face it, I'm no artist."

Mr. Mercurio opens a portfolio he has brought with him and spreads some of its contents on the table. "Here, look at some of the pieces that other students have done. Can you find one that's perfect?"

"This one is. Oh, it does have a few smudges. But these people can do a lot better work than I can. No matter how hard I try, I'm not any good at art stuff."

"Do you think these people were born knowing how to draw and paint, or did they learn how to do it with practice?"

"It seems to me that some people are just naturally better artists than others."

"So you think these people—the ones who did these pictures—don't have to put much effort into their work because they're born with artistic talent?"

"Of course they don't put much effort into it! They wouldn't be laughing and having fun during class if they had to try as hard as I do."

Mr. Mercurio looks William sternly in the eye and says, "Artistic talent comes from practice, not from heredity. You can get better only if you practice and then let me give you feedback."

Hearing no response, Mr. Mercurio stands up, then gathers the drawings and paintings he has shown William and returns them to the portfolio. "You know, it's always the perfectionists who have trouble in my class," he says as he walks away.

Note: William committed suicide on his 15th birthday.

Questions for "The Perfectionist"

1.   A **mastery goal** is a desire to gain new information or skills; a **performance goal** is a desire to be judged favorably for one's achievements. Does William have a mastery goal or a performance goal in his art class?

2.   William seems to believe that artistic ability is an inherited quality. How would you best characterize his attribution?
     a. Internal, controllable, unstable
     b. Internal, uncontrollable, stable
     c. External, uncontrollable, stable
     d. External, controllable, unstable

3.   Are Mr. Mercurio's teaching strategies likely to promote performance goals or mastery goals?

4.   Three of the following behaviors suggest that William may have learned helplessness. Which behavior is **not** indicative of learned helplessness?
     a. He dislikes being reprimanded in class.
     b. He underestimates his artistic ability.
     c. He quickly gives up despite Mr. Mercurio's encouragement.
     d. He doesn't turn in any work the following morning.

5.   What evidence do you see that William may need to be referred to the school counselor?

6.   If you were Mr. Mercurio, what strategies might you use to help William?

CASE 39
The Unmotivated Student

Marcia Thomas is a teacher intern in Ms. Egan's ninth-grade general science class. Today Marcia's university supervisor is quietly observing the class as Marcia finishes a unit on electricity. Ms. Egan is in a far corner of the room, inconspicuously grading papers at her desk while Marcia is in charge.

Two days ago the students completed a lab activity in which they created simple electromagnets. Yesterday they turned in their lab reports, and today Marcia is meeting with them individually to give them feedback on their reports. As six or seven students wait in line for their turn to speak with her, the others are supposed to be reading a chapter in the textbook and writing responses to several questions about its content. Often the line of students in front of Marcia's desk prevents her from seeing what the rest of the class is doing, but she knows that most members of her class are diligent workers who are likely to be on-task.

One exception is Jodie, who didn't turn in her lab report yesterday and apparently has no intention of doing today's assignment either. Initially she occupies herself by talking to Nina, who sits in the desk beside her. As Marcia finishes a conference with a student, she looks up, sees the two girls giggling, and admonishes them to get back to work. Nina resumes reading her textbook, but Jodie stands up and walks over to see her friend Erin. For several minutes she amuses the students at Erin's table, but then Marcia sees that she's not where she's supposed to be. "Jodie, go back to your seat and get to work," Marcia says, and then resumes her discussion with the student at her desk.

Not to be so easily corralled, Jodie wanders over to a picture of the solar system hanging on the wall and traces each planet with her finger. A few minutes later, Marcia spies her once again. "OK, Jodie, that's it! Please take your book into the hall and do your work there." Jodie ignores her directive and moves to a three-dimensional model of the human digestive system. She picks it up, holds it in front of her torso, and pantomimes eating a piece of food, "digesting" it in the plastic stomach, and moving it through the intestines. Several students snicker.

"Jodie, go into the hall *now!*" Marcia shouts. Finally Jodie obliges her, although she leaves her book behind. Through a large window in the classroom wall, she continues to entertain her peers with funny faces and body contortions. Marcia ignores her, as does Ms. Egan. When the bell rings to signal the end of class, Jodie returns to her desk to gather up her textbook and the list of questions—on which she has written only her name.

At the end of the school day, the university supervisor meets with Marcia and Ms. Egan to talk about Marcia's lesson. The three of them discuss instructional strategies and classroom management practices that do and don't seem to be working well. At one point in the conversation, the supervisor asks about Jodie, whom she has not seen in previous visits to the classroom.

"Oh, yes, *Jodie,*" Ms. Egan sighs. "Jodie's been a problem all year. She has a learning disability—she reads at about a second-grade level—but obviously there are other issues going on with her as well. Sometimes she has a student-specific aide with her, but today she didn't."

"I haven't been able to keep her on-task all year," Marcia adds. "She just doesn't want to do *anything.*"

"She never has been a very motivated student," Ms. Egan says. "I don't think there's much we can do with her." Marcia nods in agreement.

Questions for "The Unmotivated Student"

1. *What weaknesses do you see in Marcia's classroom management?*
2. *Imagine you are Marcia's university supervisor. If you want to help Marcia minimize behavior problems in future lessons, which one of the following would you be **most** likely to tell her?*
    a. *"Put all visual aids (posters, models, and so forth) out of sight."*
    b. *"Make sure you can see all of your students at all times."*
    c. *"Ask your students to do all of their reading assignments at home."*
    d. *"Never give your students more than three questions to answer in a single sitting."*
3. *Why is Jodie misbehaving? Identify two or more hypotheses.*
4. *Is Jodie an "unmotivated" student? Draw on what you know about human motivation to defend your answer.*
5. *What things would you do differently from Marcia in the day's lesson?*

CASE 40
Proofreading

When they arrive at their sophomore English composition class, Mr. Kalantari's students immediately copy into their notebooks the two sentences that the overhead projector is displaying on the wall:

> a stranger in an black suit knocked on my neighbors door and handed him a plane brown envelope

> connie my sister begined her paper route at 730 am and finish it at 845

Mr. Kalantari waits patiently for a few minutes while his students correct the two sentences for capitalization, punctuation, grammar, and spelling errors.

Then, poised at the front of the room with his red transparency marker in hand, Mr. Kalantari greets his class. "Good afternoon. It looks as if you've all made your editorial changes. Now tell me what mistakes you want me to fix in the first sentence."

"Capitalize the A before 'stranger,' " Rafael tells him.

"Turn '*an* black suit' to '*a* black suit,' " says Fern.

"Put an apostrophe between the R and S in 'neighbors,' " says Koy.

"Why isn't the apostrophe *after* the S in 'neighbors'?" Mr. Kalantari asks.

When Koy hesitates, Katie replies, "Because you're only talking about one neighbor."

"Does anyone disagree with Katie about where the apostrophe should go in 'neighbors'?" Mr. Kalantari pauses for a few seconds and looks around the room, but no one seems to have any objections to Katie's explanation. "Are there any more mistakes in the first sentence?"

"Yeah," Pam responds. "The word 'plane' is spelled wrong. It should be p-l-a-i-n."

"Good. Anything else?" The students shake their heads. "Careful," Mr. Kalantari prods them, "there's one more mistake that you've missed here. I'll give you a hint: In addition to having a capital letter at the beginning of the sentence, there's also something we need at the *end* of the sentence."

The students laugh, and several of them shout, "A period!"

"Hey, I'm looking at a bright bunch of teenagers today. OK, I think we've finally made the first sentence presentable. Now what about the second one?"

"Capitalize the C in 'connie,' and put a period at the end of the sentence," Bill suggests.

"Put commas around 'my sister,' " says Graham.

"Why do we put commas around 'my sister'?" Ron asks.

"The words 'my sister' are an appositive phrase because they identify who Connie is," Graham responds.

"Put colons after the '7' and the '8,' and put periods after the A and M in 'a-m,' " Fern says.

" 'Begined' isn't a word," adds Koy. "It should be 'began.' And 'finish' should be 'finished.' "

"All of you did a fine job correcting today's sentences," Mr. Kalantari tells his class. "Now remember to circle anything that you missed. Over a period of time, you might be able to see patterns in your errors."

"Mr. Kalantari, why do we have to correct sentences every time we come to class?" Clark asks.

"That's a good question, Clark. Does anyone have an answer?"

After a few seconds of awkward silence, Jamie raises her hand, and Mr. Kalantari nods for her to speak. "Well," she explains, "I think that correcting sentences every day helps me edit my own writing. Like, when I write my persuasive essays, I know that I have trouble with comma splices, so I watch out for them now."

"Yeah, it's nice to figure out my own mistakes instead of having a teacher point them out for me," Gary adds.

"Did that answer your question, Clark?" Mr. Kalantari asks. Clark mumbles something in affirmation, and Mr. Kalantari continues, "OK, then, let's move on to the autobiographical stories you've been working on. As I promised you yesterday, you can have 30 minutes to proofread one another's work. Help me out here—what are some key things you may want to watch out for?"

"Subject-verb agreement," Rafael offers.

"Make sure the verb tenses stay the same all the way through," Pam suggests.

"Look for places where you should have a comma or quotation marks," Ron adds.

"OK, we've gotten some good ideas in terms of grammar and punctuation," Mr. Kalantari observes. "Now what should you be looking for in terms of the *content* of the essays you're proofreading?"

"We have to make sure that everything fits together," Kirk replies. "You know—what we write should be organized and logical and stuff like that."

Mr. Kalantari nods his head in agreement. "Good, Kirk. Now then, when you're reading someone else's story, what should you do if you don't know what the author is trying to communicate?"

"How about just writing a note saying what the problem is?" Lacy says. "Or maybe putting a question mark by the confusing parts?"

"Those are excellent suggestions, Lacy. All right, let's get started. Just like you did the last time, have at least two other students proofread your work. And this time I'd like for you to use at least one proofreader whom you haven't used before. The students who proof your papers should sign their names at the top of the first page, so I know who's read what. Any questions? OK, then, find a proofreading partner and begin."

After giving his students a few minutes to tackle their proofreading task, Mr. Kalantari begins to circulate around the room to provide assistance where it might be needed. While he is helping George and Anton with the subject-verb agreement in George's story, he overhears Jamie and Marla talking about their after-school plans. As he continues working with the boys, he gently reaches over to tap Jamie's desk. Out of the corner of his eye, he sees both Jamie and Marla get back to work.

❖❖❖

After conferring with Renée about the correct order of quotation marks and a comma when they appear together in the middle of a sentence, Mr. Kalantari walks to the front of the room and writes "2" on the chalkboard. Several of the students look up to see what he is doing, then return to their work. They know that the 2 indicates their teacher's rating of the current noise level in the classroom. On Mr. Kalantari's 5-point "volume" scale, a rating between 1 and 3 is in the acceptable range.

Mr. Kalantari resumes his cycle around the classroom. As he walks by Gretchen, he notices that she is leaning backward on the two back legs of her chair. He gently touches her shoulder, and she immediately returns her chair to an upright position. "Thanks, Gretchen," he whispers.

Meanwhile, he hears Kathleen complaining to her partner, "Geez, Todd, what do *you* know about this stuff? Just sign your name and we'll call it even." Mr. Kalantari looks her in the eye, and she becomes quiet.

Mr. Kalantari asks, "Todd, what do you think of Kathleen's story?"

Todd hesitates, wondering how to be tactful. "Well, she has good grammar and spelling and stuff, but all she does is describe what people are *doing*. She needs to talk about what they're thinking and feeling, too."

"Hmmm . . . interesting observation. What suggestions do you have for Kathleen to help her out here?"

"Well, take this paragraph about her brother catching the fish. She could talk about how big the fish was. She could talk about how he felt to be fishing, or maybe how he felt catching such a puny fish in front of his friends."

"I think you've given Kathleen some good ideas about how she might strengthen her story, Todd," Mr. Kalantari says. "Don't forget to write your suggestions somewhere on her paper."

"OK, class, please return to your own seats." Mr. Kalantari waits while his students get settled, then asks, "I'm curious, why do you think I have you proofread one another's papers?"

"Because sometimes you don't feel like doing your job," Bill jokes.

Mr. Kalantari takes Bill's comment in stride, then asks his question in a different way. "What might *you* gain from reading someone else's work?"

No one seems to have an answer.

"Well, I'd like you to think about my question tonight." As the bell rings to signal the end of class, Mr. Kalantari has to raise his voice to be heard. "Remember, your final draft is due tomorrow. Don't forget to turn in your rough draft, too. Great job today. I think you all got a lot accomplished."

Questions for "Proofreading"

1. *What strategies does Mr. Kalantari use to create a productive classroom climate and promote intrinsic motivation?*

2. *Which one of the following classroom management strategies is the best example of **planning for transitions**?*
   a. *Mr. Kalantari has a task for students to do as soon as they come to class.*
   b. *Mr. Kalantari asks, "Does anyone disagree with Katie?"*
   c. *Mr. Kalantari explains why he has students correct two new sentences every day.*
   d. *Mr. Kalantari circulates around the room as his students proofread one another's stories.*
3. *What strategies does Mr. Kalantari use to keep students on-task?*
4. *On what occasions does Mr. Kalantari use positive reinforcement?*
5. *What strategies does Mr. Kalantari use to cue students about inappropriate behavior?*
6. *The students proofread one another's writing. If you consider Vygotsky's concept of **internalization**, you would be most likely to predict that the students will become _____.*
   a. *more willing to accept constructive criticism from others*
   b. *increasingly resentful of other people's opinions of their work*
   c. *increasingly dependent on others to find errors in their writing*
   d. *better able to proofread their own writing when they work independently*
7. *Is Mr. Kalantari's lesson developmentally appropriate for his students? Why or why not?*

CASE 41
Cheerleading Tryouts

As Tina sits in Ms. Roche's first-period geometry class, she thinks about this afternoon's tryouts for the varsity cheerleading squad and smiles. There is no doubt in her mind that she will gain a position on the varsity squad. After all, she's one of the most popular girls at Grosvenor High School, and she's been captain of the junior varsity cheerleaders for the past 2 years now.

Remembering that Ms. Roche has agreed to serve as coach for the varsity cheerleaders this year, Tina lingers after class to offer her assistance. "Say, Ms. Roche, I'll be glad to help you coach the new girls this year. I know all the cheers and everything, but some of the other girls are pretty clueless."

"Why, thank you, Tina," Ms. Roche responds graciously. "I'll certainly keep your offer in mind."

Wearing her junior varsity captain's uniform from last year, Tina arrives at the gymnasium after tryouts have already begun. She sees several unfamiliar young women sitting at a long table while Kara, a girl in her biology class, performs the routine she has planned. As the women observe Kara's performance, they occasionally make marks on the papers in front of them. A bit puzzled, Tina walks between the table and Kara, then plops herself down on the bleachers next to Sonya.

"Who are those people at the judges' table?" she asks Sonya.

"They're cheerleaders from State U.," Sonya replies. "Ms. Roche asked them to judge us this year so there wouldn't be so much bias in the ratings. Say, what's your tryout routine like?"

Ignoring her friend's question, Tina watches Kara and shrieks, "Get a load of those legs! Have you ever seen anything so *skinny?*" Overhearing her, Kara becomes flustered, and Tina snickers.

Ms. Roche, who has been standing on the sidelines, quickly approaches the bleachers. "Young lady!" she says sternly, looking directly at Tina. "You will keep your comments to yourself if you want to try out for a spot on my team!"

"Oh, I'm sorry," Tina responds sweetly. "I sure didn't mean to say that out loud." Then, turning to a group of students sitting behind her, she adds, "I think *everyone* should have an opportunity to try out, even if she doesn't have a snowball's chance in hell of making it."

An hour later, Tina's name is called. Tina strolls over to the judges' table and introduces herself, then performs the same routine that she used during her junior varsity tryouts last year. "I've nailed it!" she thinks. "Ha! Didn't I look good in front of everyone!"

She looks at the judges, but they aren't smiling; in fact, two of them are shaking their heads in disgust. Tina senses that something is wrong. Maybe she shouldn't have walked in front of the table during Kara's routine.

"Is that all you're going to do for us today, Tina?" one of the judges asks. "Perhaps you didn't read the memo we sent to everyone last week. At this level, we expect to see splits, forward and backward flips, and walkovers."

Tina is too stunned to respond. After whispering with the others at the table, the same judge continues, "We'll let you have one more try. Give it your best shot this time."

"*Now?*" Tina replies in dismay. She notices that many of the students sitting in the bleachers, including Miss Skinny Legs, are clearly enjoying her obvious discomfort.

"Geez, I don't know how to do a back flip," Tina thinks. "I'll look like a complete fool in front of everyone." She repeats her routine with a handstand and a forward flip, hoping that the judges won't notice that several required elements are missing. But they *do* notice, and Tina finds out later that afternoon that she hasn't made the squad.

The next day, Tina confronts Ms. Roche at the beginning of class. "It wasn't fair, you know. How was I supposed to know about the moves that were required for the tryout routine?"

"The requirements were listed in the school newspaper 2 weeks ago," Ms. Roche tells her. "They were also posted on bulletin boards throughout the school. And Ms. Bailey mentioned that there were new requirements at least three different times when she made her daily announcements over the intercom."

"It still wasn't fair. How was I supposed to change my routine in the middle of tryouts?"

Ms. Roche has little patience for Tina's unjustified fault finding. "Maybe next time you'll pay closer attention to what you're supposed to do when you try out."

"Yeah, right! And what was the deal with those judges, anyway? You should have asked people from our own school, not a bunch of off-the-wall idiots!"

"Tina, we can discuss this after class. Now is the time for geometry."

"You're a real jerk, Ms. Roche! Too bad you're not a real *roach,* too, or I'd step on you." Tina stomps to her seat. "What are *you* staring at?" she yells at several of her classmates.

Ignoring Tina, Ms. Roche says, "OK, class, before we begin today's group work, please hand in last night's homework assignment."

"I didn't have time to do it because I was wasting my time on some stupid, biased cheerleading tryout!" Tina shouts. The entire class looks at Ms. Roche to see how she will respond.

"Class, it seems that Tina is having a bad day today. I think we had all better ignore her until she gets her temper under control." Tina leans back in her chair, crossing her arms and looking defiant.

Ms. Roche tries to draw the class's attention back to her agenda for the day. "Did anyone have trouble with the problems on the homework assignment?"

"I did!" Tina shouts. "But to tell you the truth, Ms. Roche, *you* are my biggest problem! What does a *roach* know about cheerleading anyway?!!"

"Tina, you have 60 seconds to get to the counseling office." When Tina hesitates, Ms. Roche screams, "*Now!*" Tina knocks several books and spiral notebooks off other students' desks as she storms out of the room.

"Roche is a jerk!" is Tina's parting shot as she disappears from sight. Ms. Roche is visibly shaken, but she proceeds with the day's lesson without further comment on what has just transpired.

Questions for "Cheerleading Tryouts"

1. *A **mastery goal** is a desire to gain new information or skills; a **performance goal** is a desire to be judged favorably for one's achievements. Does Tina have mastery goals or performance goals when trying out for the cheerleading squad? Justify your response with examples from the case study.*
2. *Tina's behavior toward Kara can best be categorized as which one of the following?*
   a. *Self-handicapping*
   b. *Reactive aggression*
   c. *Relational aggression*
   d. *Negative reinforcement*
3. *What evidence in the case suggests that Tina has deficits in perspective taking? What evidence suggests that on some occasions she **can** take other people's perspectives?*
4. *Characterize Tina's attributions regarding her failure to make the varsity cheerleading squad.*
5. *How does Ms. Roche respond to Tina's disruptive behaviors? Are her strategies effective?*
6. *Is it a good idea to send Tina to the office? Why or why not?*
7. *If you had a student like Tina, what strategies might you use to deal with her behavior?*
8. *How might a teacher or counselor enhance Tina's perspective-taking ability?*

CASE 42
The Morning Routine

Every morning Ms. Parker's second-grade class follows a predictable routine. Each of the reading groups meets with Ms. Parker for about 20 or 30 minutes. When children are not in their reading groups, they have several tasks to accomplish at their desks: They need to write the week's spelling words 10 times each, complete three pages in their phonics workbooks, fill in a "following-directions" worksheet, and practice their addition facts.

This particular morning Seeley is confused about her spelling words. She has already learned how to spell words such as *cap, tap,* and *mad,* but now the same words seem to have the letter *e* at the end of them (*cape, tape, made*). She vaguely remembers Ms. Parker saying something yesterday about how the words this week follow the "silent *e*" rule, but she can't recall what the rule is. Instead of telling her teacher about her confusion with the new rule, she reprimands herself, "Seeley, pay attention! You need to listen more carefully!" Then she just copies each word 10 times and pulls out her phonics workbook.

For 2 weeks now, the phonics worksheets have been providing practice with consonant blends. Today's worksheets focus on *l* blends such as *pl, bl, cl,* and *fl* in words such as *plate, block, clock,* and *flower.* At the top of the first worksheet, Seeley sees a picture of a clock and the letters *o-c-k* with two blanks in front of them ("_ _ o c k"); she dutifully writes the letters *c* and *l* in the blanks. Next she sees a picture of a flower followed by "_ _ o w e r" and correctly writes *f* and *l*.

As Seeley finishes her phonics assignment, she hears her reading group being called to the reading table at the front of the room. Before the group starts reading, Ms. Parker reviews the "silent *e*" rule once again, but Seeley is still confused. "How can I read the words out loud when I must read every *e* silently?" she thinks. When it is her turn to read, she mispronounces every word that ends in silent *e,* often reading nonsensical sentences as a result. After Ms. Parker patiently corrects each mispronounced word, Seeley repeats the correct pronunciation and then continues with her reading.

Back at her desk, Seeley takes out her crayons and her following-directions worksheet. Today's sheet is similar to many others she's completed this year. This one has a line drawing of a train engine, with the numerals 1, 2, 3, and 4 inserted at different spots. At the bottom of the page is a number-color scheme: 1 = red, 2 = yellow, 3 = blue, and 4 = black. Because the scheme is always the same, Seeley knows it by heart. She first colors in all the yellow sections of the train, then the blue sections, then the red ones, and finally the black ones. She completes the task within 5 minutes.

Seeley polishes off her addition facts just as quickly. Now that she has finished her morning assignments, she knows that she has a choice between coloring quietly at her desk or going to the Listening Center at the back of the room to listen to a tape-recorded story. Today Seeley sits down at the Listening Center, puts a pair of earphones on her head, inserts a tape into the cassette player, and pushes the "play" button. Within a few minutes, she is fast asleep.

Questions for "The Morning Routine"

1. Using ideas from cognitive theories of learning, evaluate the effectiveness of Ms. Parker's morning routine.
2. How might Ms. Parker place each of the skills sets she wants her students to learn—spelling, phonics, following directions, and addition facts—within more authentic contexts?
3. Seeley continues to be confused after two explanations of the "silent e" rule. What strategies might Ms. Parker use to make sure that her students **do** understand the rule?
4. What evidence do you see that Seeley is a self-regulating learner?
5. Which one of the following strategies is most likely to help Ms. Parker's students become more self-regulating?
   a. Asking students if they understand the "silent e" rule
   b. Patiently correcting each word that a student reads incorrectly
   c. Providing learning centers at which students can work independently
   d. Providing following-directions worksheets that students can complete quickly and easily
6. Why do you think Seeley is falling asleep in class?

CASE 43
Horses and Aliens

This year Mr. Fredrickson has, for the first time, been assigning cooperative group projects in his fourth-grade class. Unfortunately, it seems as if his students have been using their group time more to socialize than to accomplish the tasks he's assigned.

"We seem to be having trouble getting work done in our cooperative groups," he tells his class one morning. "Before you meet in your regular groups today, we need to come up with some rules that might help us stay on-task. Does anyone have any suggestions?"

"Talk softly," suggests Marguerite. "Sometimes this room is so noisy that I can't even hear what the other kids in my group are saying."

"Thank you, Marguerite, that's a good start." Mr. Fredrickson writes "Cooperative Group Rules" at the top of the chalkboard, underlines it, then adds "Talk softly" immediately below.

"I think we shouldn't interrupt each other," Isaiah says. "It's like you said the other day—everyone has something to contribute. We don't interrupt when we're all together in one big group, so why should we interrupt when we're in *small* groups?"

Mr. Fredrickson adds "Don't interrupt" to the list on the chalkboard.

"We all need to help one other," Kim offers. "It shouldn't always be the same people who are doing the helping."

"Everyone should contribute to the project," Mr. Fredrickson writes. Then he says, "That reminds me, in case you haven't already noticed, I've put at least two boys and two girls in each group. That means that sometimes boys will help girls and sometimes girls will help boys. I know that a few of you want to avoid members of the opposite sex at all costs." The children laugh. "But you know what? You just might learn something from them."

Mr. Fredrickson looks at the list he's created on the chalkboard. "OK, we've established three rules for our cooperative groups. One, *talk softly*. Two, *don't interrupt*. And three, *everyone should contribute to the project*. Do these rules seem agreeable to all of you?"

"Yes," the children respond.

"So, then," Mr. Fredrickson continues, "let's talk about this afternoon's group project. I want each group to come up with a story that contains all 15 of our new spelling words. How do you think you might do this so that everyone in the group contributes?"

"We can make sure that everyone adds at least one sentence to the story," Emily proposes.

"Good idea, Emily. And how can you have everyone contribute when the group is writing its story down on paper?"

"How about if we each write our own sentences in the story?" Marguerite asks hesitantly.

"Does Marguerite's suggestion make sense to the rest of you?" Hearing no objection, Mr. Fredrickson continues, "How do you think you should begin to write your stories? Do you just pass a sheet of paper from one person to another and each do your own thing?"

"No," laughs Cecily. "First we need to decide what we want to write about. Then we can write our sentences on strips of paper and lay them out on the table."

"Do you mean that you should put them in a sequential order so the story makes sense?" asks Mr. Fredrickson.

"Yeah, that's what I mean," Cecily replies.

Mr. Fredrickson nods in approval. "So then you can copy all of the sentences onto a single sheet. All right, children, it looks as if you know how to proceed, so it's time to assemble in your groups." Familiar with the routine, the students pull out pencils and sheets of notebook paper and then move their desks to form clusters of five.

Once the noise has subsided, Mr. Fredrickson announces, "Remember, folks, at the end of the first 6 weeks, you will receive both individual grades and group grades in spelling. How do you earn your individual grades?"

"The spelling tests on Fridays!" Tomas shouts out.

"Right. And how do you earn your group grades?"

Kim raises her hand. "Whenever we do group projects, everyone gets the same grade for it."

"Right, Kim. So then I'll take the two sets of points—your Friday quiz scores and your group points—and combine them into one spelling grade. Is there anything else special about cooperative group work?"

Charlie is the first to respond. "The group that has the most points at the end of the week gets 10 minutes of free time."

"Good memory, Charlie. OK, you have 40 minutes to write your stories. I've listed the 15 spelling words on the board. Each one needs to appear in your stories at least once. Oh, yes, and be sure that you all remember to follow our new cooperative group rules."

"Let's write a story about horses," Kim suggests to her group.

"Writing about aliens from outer space would be more fun," counters Cecily. "Besides, *alien* is one of the spelling words."

"Yeah, aliens!" Bryan agrees. Bryan knows from past experience that Cecily will probably do his work for him, so it's not a bad idea to back her up.

"Horses would be better," Sean insists.

"What do you think, Robert?" Kim asks the fifth member of the group. "It should be horses, shouldn't it?"

Robert, who is terribly shy, just shrugs his shoulders and mumbles, "I don't care."

"You're being stupid!" Cecily tells Kim. "Who cares about horses? Have you ever even ridden one?"

"As a matter of fact, I *have,*" Kim retorts. "Have *you* ever seen an *alien?*"

"I think they're interesting," Cecily responds. "You do, too, Robert, don't you?"

Robert says nothing.

"Why don't we write about horses next time?" Cecily suggests as a compromise. "Besides, we'll be working together all month. Let me have my idea first, then you can have yours next time."

"How can you be so selfish?" Kim replies. "There are other people in this group besides you. Isn't that right, Robert?"

Robert watches Mr. Fredrickson work with another group. He thinks about seeking his teacher's help to get the group on-task but then decides against it.

"OK, class, you've been working for 10 minutes now," Mr. Fredrickson announces. "Your stories should be well under way, and each of you should have contributed at least one sentence by now."

"Don't be so stubborn!" Cecily scolds. "You know we'll all get zeroes if you don't help us write this alien story."

"Cecily," Kim says sternly, crossing her arms, "we'll get zeroes if *you* don't help with this story about *horses*." Sean leaves the group, walks over to Mr. Fredrickson, and pleads, "We're not getting anywhere. We need help."

Mr. Fredrickson approaches the group. "What seems to be the problem?" he asks.

"It's Cecily!" Kim shouts. "She won't do what we want."

"Yeah, *right!*" Cecily counters sarcastically. "Kim is the one who isn't cooperating. We haven't started writing our story yet, and it's all because of her."

"What are you writing about?" asks Mr. Fredrickson.

"Horses!" says Kim.

"Aliens," says Cecily. "Horses are a dumb idea."

"And aliens *aren't* dumb?" Kim asks pointedly.

"Hmmm . . . why not horses stuck in an alien world?" Mr. Fredrickson suggests. The group readily agrees and buckles down to work.

Before group time the following day, Mr. Fredrickson says, "We need to add another rule to our cooperative group rules. Does anyone have any idea what it might be?"

"Not to put one another down," says Robert. This is the first time all year that Robert has volunteered to say anything in class.

Mr. Fredrickson smiles. "Hmmm," he thinks, "maybe these cooperative groups are teaching the children more than I realized."

Questions for "Horses and Aliens"

1. *What instructional objectives might Mr. Fredrickson be trying to accomplish through the group story-writing activities?*

2. *Many fourth graders have trouble writing short stories. With this point in mind, identify several benefits that a cooperative story-writing task might have.*

3. *In what ways does Mr. Fredrickson try to follow generally recommended guidelines for facilitating productive cooperative groups?*

4.   *Which one of the following concepts related to cooperative learning is Mr. Fredrickson applying in his classroom?*
   a. *Base groups*
   b. *Peer tutoring*
   c. *Jigsaw technique*
   d. *Scripted cooperation*
5.   *Following are four different strategies that Mr. Fredrickson uses to motivate his students. Which one is most consistent with a* **cognitive perspective** *of motivation?*
   a. *He says, "Good idea, Emily."*
   b. *He gives both individual and group grades in spelling.*
   c. *He gives the groups some autonomy about how to write their stories.*
   d. *He awards 10 minutes of free time to the group with the most points.*
6.   *Mr. Fredrickson creates competition by having the groups compete for free time—a reward that will be awarded to only one group. Is this a good idea? Why or why not?*
7.   *Mr. Fredrickson intervenes when Kim and Cecily disagree about a topic for the group's story. Is this a good idea? Why or why not?*
8.   *How might a teacher keep "bossy" children such as Kim and Cecily from dominating group discussions?*

CASE 44
Endangered Species

Ms. Dennison's fifth-grade class will be spending the next 6 weeks studying endangered species in the Western Hemisphere. Ms. Dennison introduces the topic with a 25-minute videotape about manatees that live off the coast of Florida. The video depicts manatees' physical characteristics, typical habitat, social behaviors, and care of offspring; it concludes by offering the suggestions of scientists and conservationists for saving the species from extinction.

Because her students live in Wisconsin, far removed from tropical ocean waters, Ms. Dennison realizes that most of them have probably never seen manatees in the flesh. In an attempt to make the creatures more meaningful for them, she asks, "How big is a manatee compared to you?"

"It's bigger than us," Jon responds. "It's probably about the size of my mom or dad."

"It's about two of me," Marty says.

"No, I think it's more like three or four of us squashed together but a little taller," Keri suggests.

"Is a manatee like anything you've ever seen before, Keri?" Ms. Dennison asks.

"No . . . well, yeah . . . maybe," Keri replies. "It reminds me of a cow, only it lives in water. 'Cause it looks fat and is shaped like a cow's body, but it's just missing its legs."

"Excellent observation, Keri," Ms. Dennison says. "Did you know that manatees are sometimes called *water cows* or *sea cows?* Adult manatees can grow to 12 or 13 feet in length and can weigh about 3,500 pounds. Unfortunately, because they usually live in such a polluted environment, most of them grow only to about 10 feet in length and weigh about 1,000 pounds." Changing the subject, she continues, "The video told us that manatees come up to the water's surface to breathe air. But they don't have any legs, do they? So how do you think they move around in the water?"

"They use their flippers to swish themselves through the water," answers John.

"They use their tails to push themselves," adds Chase.

"When they're on the bottom, they use their flippers like legs," Keri suggests rather tentatively.

"Those are three very good hypotheses," Ms. Dennison observes. "Yesterday I went to the school library and borrowed a book about manatees. Chapter 3 tells us exactly how manatees move themselves around in the water. Who would like to read it aloud for us?"

After a lengthy discussion of manatees, Ms. Dennison says, "We need to have a system for keeping track of all the things we learn about each of the species we'll be studying." She draws her students' attention to a large matrix she has drawn on the chalkboard at the side of the room. The columns of the matrix are all labeled: *Species, Description, Habitat, Population Estimates, Feeding, Offspring, Social Behavior,* and *Causes of Mortality.* She writes "manatees" in the *Species* column, and then she and her students discuss what to write under each of the other headings.

Once the class has filled in the *manatees* row in the matrix, Ms. Dennison passes out black-and-white maps of the Western Hemisphere, depicting the borders of different countries as well as major rivers and mountain ranges. "We'll use these to indicate where each of our endangered species lives," she explains. "Take out your colored pencils, and use your blue pencil to color in the places where manatees live."

Two days later, Ms. Dennison introduces another endangered species, the logger-head turtle. She shows a short videotape depicting the habitat and behaviors of loggerhead turtles and then says, "Let's fill in another row of our endangered species matrix." She writes "loggerhead turtles" in the *Species* column, then tapes a colorful picture of a loggerhead in the *Description* column.

"When we were studying manatees," Ms. Dennison says, "we learned a new vocabulary word that refers to where a species lives. Can anyone remember what that word was?"

"Habitat!" Sally shouts out.

Ms. Dennison nods her approval. "Yes, the *habitat* of a species is the kind of environment in which its members typically live. For example, do they live on land or in water? Is the temperature warm or cold? If the species lives in water, is it fresh water or salt water? Is the habitat of loggerhead turtles the same as the habitat of manatees?"

"Loggerheads live where the manatees live," Jon responds. "Around Florida, in the Caribbean Sea, and as far north as Canada."

"Hmmm . . . what do the rest of you think?" Ms. Dennison asks.

"They can't live near Canada," Jacinda responds, "because the water's too cold."

"I'm confused, Jacinda," Ms. Dennison says. "Who are *they*—the manatees or the turtles?"

"The manatees."

"Right. Manatees live only in warm water, but loggerhead turtles can live in either warm or cold water. And unlike manatees, who stay close to shore, sea turtles migrate to the open ocean, often traveling hundreds or even thousands of miles to a beach where they can lay their eggs. *Migrate* is a new vocabulary word. What do you suppose it means?"

"Move," answers Beth.

"Yes, *migrate* means to move from one place to another. Some species migrate with the seasons. For example, many birds fly south in the fall and then fly back north again in the spring. It would be a good idea to add *migration* to your list of new vocabulary words for this week. Remember to write down a definition to help your-self remember what it means." She pauses to give the children time to write the new word in their notebooks.

"So loggerhead turtles *migrate*," Ms. Dennison continues. "Now pull out the maps of the Western Hemisphere that I gave you the other day. You've already colored your maps in blue for the manatees. Let's use red to mark where sea turtles live and migrate. Once we've found out where different endangered species live, we can start talking about how we might protect their environments so that they can grow and flourish."

Note: The following year, Ms. Dennison's class "adopted" a whale named Sophie, raising $5,000 by selling T-shirts with Sophie's picture silk-screened on the front. A local television station televised their donation to the Wildlife Federation. The enterprise was so successful that adoptions of endangered species became annual events at Ms. Dennison's school.

Questions for "Endangered Species"

1. *What strategies does Ms. Dennison use to promote students' learning? In what way is each strategy beneficial?*
2. *Which one of the following is the best example of an authentic activity?*
   a. *Watching a videotape about loggerhead turtles*
   b. *Comparing the sizes of manatees versus people*
   c. *Adopting a whale and raising money for its care*
   d. *Filling in blank cells in the matrix on the board*
3. *In responding to a question about the habitat of loggerhead turtles, Jon says, "Loggerheads live where the manatees live. Around Florida, in the Caribbean Sea, and as far north as Canada." Why does Ms. Dennison ask the other students to comment on this response?*

CASE 45
Climate

Ms. Marotta is a teacher education student who, in preparation for her teaching internship next year, is now spending 2 hours every morning observing and assisting in a middle school geography class. At the request of her supervising teacher, Mr. Koehn, she's prepared a lesson about climate using the same interactive, question-answer format that she has watched Mr. Koehn use so effectively over the past few weeks. Ms. Marotta has just led the students through their geography textbook's chapter on climate and is now beginning to engage them in a follow-up discussion.

"How many of you have air conditioning?" she asks. About half of the students raise their hands.

"If you lived in Houston instead of here in Colorado, how many of you would have air conditioning?" All but two of the students raise their hands.

Ms. Marotta glances briefly at her lesson plan. "Who can tell me what topic we talked about last Friday?"

"Temperature," says Germaine.

"Wind," says Marsha.

"Climate," says Tomas.

"OK. On Friday, Mr. Koehn described several different things that affect climate. Who can tell me what they are?" When the students remain silent, Ms. Marotta asks, "What's the difference between where we are and Long's Peak?" (Long's Peak is a nearby mountain that is more than 14,000 feet high.)

"Long's Peak is higher," Marsha says.

"Oh, yeah—*elevation!*" shouts Caitlin.

"Right, Caitlin. Elevation is one thing that affects climate. What's another one?"

"Latitude," Maya responds.

"Right. What effect does living near the water have?"

Janina whispers briefly to the girl sitting beside her and then raises her hand. "Cooler in summer, warmer in winter."

"Good, Janina. Water makes things cooler in the summer and warmer in the winter. All right, class, now open your books to page 48. Kevin, can you read the section called 'Polar Region' for us?"

Kevin is slow to find the section that Ms. Marotta is referring to. As he reads, he mumbles so much that hardly anyone can hear him. Too late, Ms. Marotta remembers that Kevin is one of the poorest readers in the class. "That's OK," she thinks. "The others can read the passage to themselves anyway."

"Who has good handwriting?" Ms. Marotta asks. "OK, Jackson, you can be our recorder today." Jackson approaches the chalkboard smiling, obviously relishing the fact that he will be the center of attention for the next few minutes. He picks up a piece of chalk, poised to begin his recording duties.

"What are some things we've just learned about the polar region?" Ms. Marotta asks. "Jackson will write your answers on the board."

"Less sunlight," says Meghan.

"Especially in winter," Julian adds.

"The ground stays frozen," says Alan.

"Long, cold winters," says Will.

"Short summer," says B.J.

"*Cool* summer," says Reynelda.

"Did you get everything on the list?" Ms. Marotta asks Jackson. "Good, I see that you did. OK, is there anything else we need to add?"

The students search their textbooks for other possibilities. "Not much precipitation!" shout Germaine and Tomas simultaneously.

"Why isn't there much precipitation?" Ms. Marotta asks.

"Because the air's so cold that it can't hold much moisture," Libby responds.

"So if you lived in Alaska, you'd have some days with very little sunlight and very long nights. What do you think it would be like to live in Alaska in the winter? How do you think you might feel?"

"Tired," says Alan.

"Lazy," says Meghan.

Ms. Marotta waits a few seconds, but the students seem to have run out of ideas. "You might get very depressed, too, mightn't you?" Several students nod. "OK. Now, who would like to read the section about the 'Temperate Region' for us?"

The lesson continues as the class reads about temperate, subtropical, and tropical regions. As the students list the characteristics of each climatic region aloud, Jackson writes them on the board.

Glancing at her watch, Ms. Marotta realizes that the class period is almost over. "Thank you for taking notes for us, Jackson," she says. "Now did you all get the characteristics of the different regions in your notebooks?"

The students look at her with blank expressions. As she surveys the room, she realizes that none of the students has even opened a notebook. Early in the school year, Mr. Koehn had the class create a section in their loose-leaf notebooks called "Geography." Why has it not occurred to anyone to take notes today? After all, Jackson has made the job easy for them by listing everything on the board.

As Ms. Marotta thinks about it, she recalls how Mr. Koehn has always told the class when to take notes and exactly what to write each time. "I guess I still have a lot to learn about teaching middle school students," she concludes.

Questions for "Climate"

1. *If you had to categorize Ms. Marotta's instructional method, which one of the following labels would you be most likely to use?*
   a. Mastery learning
   b. Discovery learning

      c. Reciprocal teaching

      d. Expository instruction

2. *If you were to apply Howard Gardner's theory of multiple intelligences in analyzing the lesson, on which intelligence would you conclude the lesson most heavily depends?*

      a. Linguistic

      b. Naturalist

      c. Intrapersonal

      d. Interpersonal

3. *If you were to look at the lesson from the perspective of Bloom's taxonomy, on which two levels does Ms. Marotta focus most of her efforts?*

4. *What strengths do you see in Ms. Marotta's lesson?*

5. *What weaknesses do you see in Ms. Marotta's lesson?*

6. *Ms. Marotta inadvertently asks Kevin, a poor reader, to read a section of the chapter aloud. Is this a good idea? Why or why not?*

7. *Why do the students not take notes even though Jackson has made it easy for them to do so?*

8. *Good teachers reflect on how their lessons have gone. Was Ms. Marotta's post-class reflection likely to be helpful to her? Why or why not?*

9. *Suggest two alternative approaches Ms. Marotta might use in teaching one or more concepts related to climate.*

10. *Most middle school students are poor note takers and have few other effective study skills. Suggest three different things Ms. Marotta might do to foster more effective learning and studying.*

11. *Describe three different assessment techniques Ms. Marotta might use to assess students' understanding of what they have learned. Base your response on principles of effective assessment.*

CASE 46
The Research Paper

As Mr. Van Holten begins his fifth year teaching seventh-grade English, he reflects back on the worksheets and one-page compositions he has assigned in previous years. He realizes that those assignments have had little relevance to the real-world tasks that his students will eventually face. He decides to assign a more meaningful, authentic task this year by asking his students to write a 10-page research paper on a topic of their choice, with the paper being due at the end of the school year.

Judging from past experience, Mr. Van Holten knows that some of his students will have limited writing skills, so he decides to ease his classes into the writing process with a series of short writing assignments. He begins fall semester by having his students write three sentences every day. He wants writing to be an enjoyable activity, not an unpleasant one, so he refrains from giving them any feedback about spelling and grammar errors. Instead, he simply puts checkmarks in his grade book to indicate completed assignments.

After 2 weeks of daily sentence writing, Mr. Van Holten introduces a new task: During each class period, students must write a short paragraph that has a topic sentence and at least three supporting sentences. Continuing to believe that negative feedback would dampen students' motivation to write, he again provides no feedback about the quality of work that is produced.

Two weeks later, Mr. Van Holten changes the daily task once again. Each day students must choose a specific topic and write three paragraphs about it. In addition, he now insists that everyone use correct spelling.

The following month, Mr. Van Holten asks his students to write a five-paragraph theme once a week. First drafts of these themes are due every Wednesday. On Thursday, the students exchange papers and check one another's work for mechanical errors. Final drafts are due at the beginning of class each Friday. Any spelling or grammatical errors on these final drafts will lower a student's grade for the assignment by 10%. Mr. Van Holten's students continue to write these theme papers until the end of the semester.

On the first day of spring semester, Mr. Van Holten teaches his students how to use such references as encyclopedias, magazines, CD-ROMs, and online resources. The following day, he describes the major assignment for the semester: a 10-page research paper that will be worth 75% of the final semester grade.

When many students express concern that they don't have the ability to write such a long paper, Mr. Van Holten reassures them. "Of course you can do this assignment, folks. You spent all of last semester practicing the kind of writing that you will be doing. Besides, I'll give you lots of time in class to work on your papers, and I'll help you during that time if you ask me to. And you can go to the library whenever you need to."

Over the next few weeks, Mr. Van Holten notices that although some of his students are taking advantage of the allotted class time to work on their papers, other students are wasting time socializing or completing homework for other classes. He decides to ignore the off-task behaviors, rationalizing that students must take responsibility for their own learning. If they don't finish their papers, then they will simply suffer the logical consequence—a failing grade.

On the day the research papers are due, Mr. Van Holten receives a motley assortment of products from his students, including all of the following:

- Completed papers, either typed or handwritten, that meet the general criteria described at the beginning of the semester (i.e., 10 pages, with a focus on a single research topic)
- Uncompleted papers that are partially typed and partially handwritten
- Papers plagiarized from original sources
- Papers listing many unrelated facts written in the form of paragraphs
- Rambling compositions without any references
- Notes from the parents of several of the more "chatty" students explaining why the work is incomplete

Mr. Van Holten has no idea how he should grade his students' papers. Does he grade them solely on content? Should he also consider such factors as grammar and punctuation? Should he give the same credit for papers that are typed, handwritten, or a mixture of the two? He has never explained that plagiarism is unacceptable, so should he penalize those students who have copied their papers word for word from library books or Internet Web sites? He has neglected to teach students how to use footnotes to reference others' ideas, so should he deduct points when students haven't included references? Should he give the "chatty" students a few more days to complete their papers at home? Mr. Van Holten is at a complete loss as to what to do.

Questions for "The Research Paper"

1. *Mr. Van Holten uses some strategies that are consistent with Vygotsky's theory of cognitive development and others that are not. Which one of the following is **least** consistent with Vygotsky's ideas?*
   a. *Assisting students as they work on their papers in class*
   b. *Giving credit for early assignments regardless of their quality*
   c. *Asking students to exchange papers and check one another's work for mechanical errors*
   d. *Easing students into the writing process with a series of increasingly complex writing assignments*
2. *What mistakes does Mr. Van Holten make?*

3. *In the early weeks of the school year, Mr. Van Holten gives his students no feedback about grammar and spelling. Is this decision a good one? Why or why not?*

4. *What strategies might Mr. Van Holten use to scaffold the difficult task that he has assigned?*

5. *What strategies might Mr. Van Holten use to keep students on-task during the second semester?*

6. *How might students with cognitive disabilities and other special educational needs have performed on Mr. Van Holten's assignment?*

7. *How should Mr. Van Holten evaluate his students' papers?*

8. *In **criterion-referenced assessment,** a teacher evaluates a student's performance relative to predetermined standards or criteria. In **norm-referenced assessment,** a teacher evaluates a student's performance in terms of how it compares with that of the student's peers. Should Mr. Van Holten take a criterion-referenced or a norm-referenced approach in grading the research papers? Justify your choice.*

CASE 47
The Pearl

Mr. Hartman's eleventh-grade English class is reviewing for a test on John Steinbeck's *The Pearl,* the novel it's been reading for the past 2 weeks. To help focus the review session, Mr. Hartman has written four terms on the board: *Setting, Theme, Conflict,* and *Symbolism.* Most of his students have their notebooks open in front of them, ready to take notes they can use when they study this evening.

"We've talked about *setting* before, haven't we?" says Mr. Hartman. "It's when and where a story takes place. What's the setting for *The Pearl?*"

Trin Lee raises her hand. "It starts out in a small village, then ends up in the mountains. Because it's a parable, time doesn't exist. It takes place sometime in the past, but we don't know exactly when."

"Great answer, Trin Lee!" Mr. Hartman writes "village and mountains; time is in the past" to the right of *Setting* on the board. He waits until his students have had time to copy what he's written and then asks, "Can anyone add anything to the setting?" When no one responds, he says, "OK, then let's discuss the theme of the story. Who can tell me what a *theme* is?"

"It's the main idea of the story—the underlying message," Rusty replies. "There's a 'C' word you used to describe it yesterday—*coots* or *croots* or something like that."

"I think the term I used yesterday was *crux,*" Mr. Hartman says as he writes the word on the board. "*Crux* is another way of saying 'main idea.' So what is *The Pearl*'s theme?"

"It's man's inhumanity to man," Loraine volunteers. "The pearl buyers are part of a conspiracy to cheat the divers out of their money. The doctor and the priest take advantage of the poor people."

"But there's more to it than that," Jean-Luc points out. "Steinbeck was talking about why materialism is so bad. I think he was warning us that we only hurt ourselves when we get greedy."

"You're on the right track, Jean-Luc," Mr. Hartman says. "Tell us a little bit more about what you mean."

"Well, Kino's search for wealth destroyed his happiness. He ruined his simple, happy life because of his greed."

"So in this novel we have two themes: people's inhumanity toward one another and the corruptive influence of materialism." Mr. Hartman writes both phrases on the board next to *Theme* and then continues, "Who can tell us about the *conflict* of the story?"

"I can," Meg offers. "The conflict is whether to trust your own judgment or go see what an expert thinks. For example, when the scorpion stung the baby, the parents knew what to do and they did it—they sucked the poison out of the baby's wound. Yet they weren't sure they did the right thing, so they went to the doctor afterwards to get his advice."

"So the conflict is 'trusting oneself versus trusting an expert,' " Mr. Hartman says aloud as he writes the phrase on the board next to *Conflict*. "Finally, what are some of the *symbols* in the story?"

"Steinbeck uses dark and light imagery," Daniel replies. "Light symbolizes good, and darkness symbolizes evil."

"True," says Mr. Hartman, "but what about the title of the book? What do you think the pearl is a symbol of?"

"It represents Kino's hopes and dreams," Rob replies. "He thinks that finding a pearl is the only way he can change his life. It's sorta like winning the lottery for us."

"Nice analogy, Rob," responds Mr. Hartman. "Do you think the pearl might also be a symbol for something else as well?"

"It's evil for Kino and Juana," Leigh suggests, "because if Kino hadn't found the pearl, they'd probably still be happy."

"Good answer, Leigh," Mr. Hartman replies as he writes "good and evil, hopes and dreams" on the board next to *Symbolism*. "It looks to me as if you people are ready for tomorrow's test. Any questions?" The students shake their heads and close their notebooks as the final bell rings.

The next day, Mr. Hartman waits for his students to clear their desks of everything but their pencils, then he hands out the test. "You have 35 minutes to take the test. There are 10 matching items where you match people in the book with personality traits. Then there are 10 true-false items regarding things that did or did not happen in the story. After that, there are 20 multiple-choice items related to specific details in the plot and 10 more related to new vocabulary words."

A few minutes later, Loraine gets up and approaches Mr. Hartman's desk. "I don't understand this question," she whispers. She points to the following item on the second page:

When Kino looks at the pearl for the last time, he thinks it is:
    a. evil
    b. wonderful
    c. a dream
    d. a keepsake

"I have it in my notes that he sees the pearl both as evil and as a dream," she continues. "So which letter should I circle?"

"I can't tell you that," Mr. Hartman says. "Just choose the best one."

"But they're *both* true!"

"You're wasting too much time on one question, Loraine. You have only 10 minutes to finish the test. Why don't you leave this question for now and come back to it later if you have time?"

Obviously frustrated, Loraine leaves her teacher's desk. Meanwhile, Elena walks to the front of the room. "Mr. Hartman," she says, "we never talked about this stuff." She points to an item at the bottom of the second page:

A real pearl is created by:
    a. chemical transformation
    b. a grain of sand
    c. a grain of salt
    d. a protective secretion

"It was in the novel, Elena," Mr. Hartman replies. "You'll have to figure it out by yourself." Elena is clearly unhappy as she returns to her seat.

"Man, this is stupid!" Nellie whispers to Booker, who is sitting across the aisle from her. "We never even discussed vocabulary words."

"I can't remember some of these characters," Booker whispers back. "They weren't important for the story, so we never talked about them in class."

"Hey, shut up, you guys!" Alex complains.

"Enough talking," Mr. Hartman admonishes the class. "Audrey, try to keep your eyes on your own paper. People, you're making this test harder than it needs to be. I'm not going to tell you any of the answers. I want you to stay in your seats and just try your best. You have only 5 more minutes to finish up, then we need to begin our discussion of *To Kill a Mockingbird*."

The following Monday Mr. Hartman gives his students their graded test papers. "I'm not at all pleased with your test performance," he complains. "None of you did very well on the new vocabulary words that appeared in the novel."

"But we never expected anything about vocabulary on the test," Elena complains. "Like, who would know what *escarpment* means?"

"Well, now you know that you need to study new vocabulary words the next time we have a test," Mr. Hartman replies. "Many of you confused the pearl buyer and the doctor in the matching section—the doctor was the "selfish man" and the pearl buyer was the "shrewd appraiser," not the other way around. And all of you missed items 7 and 9 on the true-false. Fortunately, most of you did fine on the multiple-choice questions."

"Since we all missed some of the same questions, are you going to throw them out?" Tobey asks.

"No, I want to base the test scores on 100 points," Mr. Hartman replies. "I can't do that if we throw out some of the questions."

"Mr. Hartman, I'm confused," Trin Lee says. "Why did we go over themes and symbolism and stuff like that if the test was over picky details?"

"Well, it's a good idea to know that stuff. The test I gave you yesterday was specially designed by experts at a company in California. I knew it would be a better test than I could ever make up myself."

"So you didn't write the test yourself?" Trin Lee asks, seeking clarification.

"That's correct. I will be using tests written by the same experts for the other novels we read this semester. So if you didn't do as well as you'd like on this first test, at least you know what to expect on the next one."

Questions for "The Pearl"

1. *Given how Mr. Hartman conducts his lesson on Steinbeck's The Pearl, he appears to be assuming that his students have capabilities consistent with which one of Piaget's stages?*
   a. *Concrete operations*
   b. *Formal operations*
   c. *Preoperational*
   d. *Sensorimotor*
2. *What effective instructional strategies does Mr. Hartman use during his lesson?*
3. *On what occasions does either Mr. Hartman or a student encourage elaboration as a cognitive process?*
4. *Why does Rusty have trouble remembering the word **crux?***
5. *In what way does Rob contribute to the class's understanding of The Pearl?*
6. *Which one of the following terms best describes the kind of assessment Mr. Hartman uses to assess his students' mastery of content related to The Pearl?*
   a. *Informal*
   b. *Authentic*
   c. *Formative*
   d. *Summative*
7. *The **validity** of an assessment instrument is the extent to which it actually assesses what it is intended to assess. Is Mr. Hartman's test a valid one? Why or why not?*
8. *The **reliability** of an assessment instrument is the extent to which it consistently yields similar results. Is Mr. Hartman's test a reliable one? Why or why not?*
9. *The students complain that the test does not reflect the things they've learned in class. What other problems do you see in Mr. Hartman's test?*
10. *If you were Mr. Hartman, what other strategies might you use to have students demonstrate their understanding of The Pearl?*

CASE 48
Under the Bleachers

Thad Buchanan, a senior at Monroe High School, has just learned that the local Kiwanis Club has awarded him a large scholarship to attend college next year, provided that he maintains the 3.0 average he currently has and earns at least a C in all of his classes. Thad knows that he will be the first member of his family to attend college. His parents are very proud of him, and he certainly doesn't want to let them down. But the new scholarship has him worried; he's been struggling in Ms. Ihlenfeldt's calculus class, and he's afraid that he's going to finish the year with a D.

Ms. Ihlenfeldt knows that the scholarship is very important to Thad because his parents can't possibly afford to send him to college. So she has gladly been giving him extra help after school each day. She's also been assigning extra problems for him to do on the weekends so that he can gain additional practice with concepts and procedures that seem to give him particular difficulty. Thad is grateful for his teacher's assistance, and he works hard to make the most of both the tutoring and the homework assignments that she gives him.

The day of his first calculus test, Thad thinks he is prepared but doesn't want to take any chances. He writes all the formulas he thinks he will need on a small note card and then hides the card up his sleeve. As he begins the test, he realizes that he can remember the formulas on his own. But when he finishes, he slips out the note card just to double-check his work.

"Thad, what are you *doing??!!*" Ms. Ihlenfeldt is standing over him, and all of his classmates are looking in his direction.

"I . . . umm . . . I was just checking my answers. I swear I didn't use this during the test, Ms. Ihlenfeldt!"

"Yeah, *right!*" whispers Jill, who is sitting behind him.

"You're busted, man," Tyrone mutters. "You've been caught red-handed. You might as well admit it."

As Ms. Ihlenfeldt takes the note card from Thad's hand, he pleads, "I wasn't cheating! I swear it!"

"Hey, come on, Thad!" Quinton exclaims. "If you had a cheat sheet anywhere *near* the test, then you were cheating. Ms. Ihlenfeldt grades her tests on a curve. It's not fair for the rest of us to get bad grades just because you cheated."

"Yeah, Thad, what were you going to do—change your *wrong* answers?" Jason taunts.

"No, no! It wasn't like that. I was just checking my work!" Obviously very upset, Thad runs out of the room.

"OK, everyone," Ms. Ihlenfeldt tells the class, "please get back to work and finish your tests. I'll deal with Thad after class."

"What's to deal with?" Stewart asks. "Everyone knows the school policy. Students who are caught cheating automatically flunk and have to take the course over. I know, because it happened to me."

During her planning period the following hour, Ms. Ihlenfeldt goes in search of Thad. She knows him well enough to guess that he's gone out by the football field behind the school building. Sure enough, that's where she finds him, sitting alone under the bleachers with his head in his hands. Quietly, she sits down beside him.

"What happened, Thad?"

"I've blown it, haven't I?"

"I don't know yet. I *do* know that you were ready for the test. Why did you think you had to cheat?"

"Last night I panicked. I felt all this pressure. I just didn't want to let anyone down. So I brought a crutch. And now it's ruined me."

"*Who* didn't you want to let down?"

"You, my parents, my brothers and sisters, my Uncle Jake—everyone. All they keep saying is, 'Look at Thad. Isn't he great? The first Buchanan to go to college.' Why do I have to be the *first?*"

"Thad, I think that the person you let down the most is yourself. You're the one you've really hurt here."

"No, that's not true. I've let you down after all the time and help you've given me. I've let my family down after they've been so proud of me. Most of all, I've proven that I'm not good enough to go to college."

"Thad, you have proven to me time after time that you understand calculus very well. There was no doubt in my mind today that you would do well on the test. I wonder if maybe you actually set yourself up to fail here."

"What?"

"I wonder if maybe you were afraid of doing well—if maybe you thought that Buchanans don't belong in college."

"Yeah . . . I guess it's *true.* I mean, what makes me so special? I thought my education would be a slap in my dad's face . . . as if I'm better than he is somehow."

"You've had more educational opportunities than your parents had when they were your age, but that doesn't mean you're better than they are. What it really means is that you've been more *fortunate.*"

"Oh . . . I guess I never thought of it that way."

"Why did you bring the note card, Thad?"

"I was afraid of letting everyone down."

"Any other reason?"

"I . . . I was afraid I'd pass. If I passed, then I'd be better than my family . . . my parents. I didn't want to insult them . . . you know, their lack of education and all."

Ms. Ihlenfeldt is astounded by Thad's ability to reflect on his own behavior. She probes him further. "Do you really think your parents would feel insulted if you were to get a college degree?"

"Yeah . . . well, no. I guess it sounds kinda stupid, doesn't it?"

"Thad, come back to my classroom after school. I'll let you take the test again, but without your note card this time."

"Is it really fair to the rest of the class? The school says I have to flunk."

"Thad, do you want to go to college?"

"Yes, more than anything."

"Why, Thad? *Why* do you want to go to college?"

"Because I want to prove to myself that I can do it . . . that I'm smart enough to get a college degree."

"Thad, the school policy is designed to teach students a lesson—that cheating is not in your own best interest over the long run. I think you've already learned that lesson."

"Thanks, Ms. Ihlenfeldt . . . for everything," Thad tells his teacher as he turns in his completed test. Once he's left the room, Ms. Ihlenfeldt grades his work. She's delighted to discover that he's earned an almost perfect score—96% correct.

Note: Four and a half years later, Thad graduated from M.I.T. with a degree in engineering. He took a job with a computer firm in New England and often wrote to Ms. Ihlenfeldt to let her know how he was doing.

Questions for "Under the Bleachers"

1. *Thad will be the first person in his family to attend college. Describe strategies Ms. Ihlenfeldt uses to encourage and support Thad in his efforts in her class. Also identify other strategies teachers might use with future first-generation college students.*

2. *Quinton says, "Ms. Ihlenfeldt grades her tests on a curve." Which one of the following statements most accurately describes her approach?*
    a. *She engages in formative (rather than summative) evaluation.*
    b. *She engages in norm-referenced (rather than criterion-referenced) evaluation.*
    c. *She places higher priority on validity than on reliability in her assessment techniques.*
    d. *She places higher priority on reliability than on validity in her assessment techniques.*

3. *Ms. Ihlenfeldt tells Thad, "I wonder if maybe you actually set yourself up to fail here." In this statement, she is suggesting that Thad _____.*
    a. *engaged in self-handicapping*
    b. *has a low sense of self-worth*

       c. *was a victim of self-socialization*

       d. *has a poorly developed theory of mind*

4. *If you were Thad's teacher, would you allow him to retake the test? Why or why not?*

5. *In general, what are the advantages and disadvantages of allowing students to retake an exam?*

6. *Is it appropriate for schools to punish cheating in the way that Monroe High School does (i.e., by awarding an automatic F to all offenders)? Why or why not?*